CRAFT SMART

QED Publishing

QED Project Editor: Ruth Symons

Created for QED Publishing by Tall Tree Ltd
Editor: Catherine Saunders
Designers: Jonathan Vipond and Marisa Renzullo
Illustrator: Geraint Ford and Barry Croucher
Photography: Michael Wicks

First published in the UK in 2013 by
QED Publishing, a Quarto Group company
The Old Brewery, 6 Blundell Street,
London, N7 9BH

www.qed-publishing.co.uk

A catalogue record for this book is available from the British Library.

ISBN 978 1 78171 534 5

Printed in China

Picture credits
(t=top, b=bottom, l=left, r=right, c=centre, fc=front cover, bc=back cover)
Shutterstock: Africa Studio, 42tr, 49r, 63tr, 66r; Albo003, 35bl; Alexandr Makarov, fcl; Andrey_Kuzmin, 46t; April70, 56bl; bengy, 51bl; Bennyartist, 67, 69, 71, 73, 75, 77, 79, 81, 83, 85, 87, 89; Blacknote, 56tr; bociek666, 34br; CLM, 70tr, 90tl, 90r, 102r; Crepesoles, fc; cristi180884, 62r; DenisNata, 10tr; design56, 14c; Diana Taliun, 68bl; dogboxstudio, 78tr; Dulce Rubia, 40b; duniascrap; Elena Itsenko 18r; elen_studio, 51br; Evyatar Dayan, 46tr; Feng Yu, 63l; Garsya, fc, 34r; Getideaka 6tr; gorillaimages, 51bc; Hein Nouwens, 44c; holbox, 51bc; Homydesign, 35tl; Horiyan, 35tc; Iakov Filimonov, 68r, 80tr; IDAL, 98c; Ilya Akinshin, 72l; infografick, 6l; Ingvar Bjork, 54cr; Irina Nartova, fc, 8, 11, 13, 15, 17, 19, 21, 23, 25, 27, 29, 31, 33; Iryna1, 115r; Ivancovlad, 112l; Iwona Grodzka, fc; jabiru, fc, 7br; jeka84, 77tr; Jim Hughes, 62tr, 86tr; Jiri Hera, 51bc; KariDesign, 34bc; Katrina Leigh, 52t, 53tr; Kitch Bain, fcl; Konstanttin, 35bl; kuma, 78tl, bl; kzww, 90tr; Larina Natalia, 3tc; Luis Carlos Jimenez del rio, 34tr; MaPaSa, fc; Madlen, 46, 98t, 112r; magicoven, 7b, 63b; Magnia, 56br; Mighty Sequoia Studio, 6bl; s1001, 6b; Nattika, fcl, bccl, 62br; NinaMalyna, fc; Odua Images, fc; oksana2010, 34l; oksix, 62l; olga.lolipops, 35bl; OlyaSenko, 90–118 bl/br; optimarc, fc; PhotoHouse, fc; Picsfive, fc, 100c; pukach, fc, 40c, 55r, 58tr; S1001, 34bl; s73, 92, 95, 97, 99, 101, 102, 107, 109, 111, 113, 115, 117; Shutswis, 34tc, 42cr; Sirikorn Techatraibhop, 7rc; Skazka Grez, 6br; SmileStudio, 7tl; spillikin, 14r; steckfigures, 56bc; Tatiana Volgutova, 74r; Thomas Klee, 108r; Vaclav Mach, 63r; valzan, fc; Veronika Mannova, 35tr; Victorian Traditions, 35bl; victoriaKh, 100rc; violetblue, 30r; Vodoleyka, 106r, 110r; Vysokova Ekaterina, 102c; YaiSirichai, 6.

At the top of the page for each project you will find this handy key. It will tell you the difficulty level to expect from each project:

Quick creative fix

These projects are quick, easy and perfect for a beginner.

Sharpen your skills

Confident with your beginner skills? Move onto these slightly tougher projects.

Ready for a challenge

For a challenging project you can really get stuck into.

Creative masterpiece

Think you can tackle the toughest creative projects? Have a go at these.

Note to Adults:
Some children might be able to do some or all of these projects on their own, while others might need more help. These are projects that you can work on together, not only to avoid any problems or accidents, but also to share in the fun of making crafts.

In preparation of this book, all due care has been exercised with regard to the activities and advice depicted. The publishers regret that they can accept no liability for any loss or injury sustained.

CRAFT
SMART

Adel Kay • Danielle Lowy • Michelle Powell • Laura Torres

QED Publishing

CONTENTS

PAPERCRAFT

RECYCLING

JEWELLERY

KNITTING

PAPERCRAFT MATERIALS

Tissue paper
This thin paper is ideal for creating delicate effects, such as flower petals, and for découpage (see page 14).

Crêpe paper
Crêpe paper has been wrinkled up and then flattened, so it is slightly stretchy. It is great for covering objects.

crêpe paper

Newspaper
Newspaper is great for papier mâché because it is cheap, easy to tear and absorbs the glue well.

Origami paper
You can cut any thin paper into a square for origami. You can also buy square origami paper.

origami paper

Scrapbooking paper
Patterned papers made for scrapbooking are often thicker than ordinary paper, so they are ideal for paper sculptures.

Card
Card is thicker than paper and comes in lots of different weights and colours. Thin card is great for paper crafts, while thicker card is often used as the base for other crafting projects.

Recycled paper
Old paper cups, plates, envelopes, magazines and wrapping paper can all be reused in your craft projects, as well as old cardboard tubes and boxes.

cardboard boxes

newspapers

scrapbooking paper

tissue paper

6

old cardboard tubes

quilling tool

scoring tool

Glue

All-purpose glue works quickly and sticks different surfaces together well. PVA glue can be watered down and used as varnish.

Glitter glue

This is glitter mixed with glue to make it easy to apply. Make sure you let it dry properly, otherwise it might smudge.

Stick-on gemstones

These sparkly plastic jewels come with glue on the back, so they are easy to add to your projects.

Paint

Thick poster paint or acrylic paint is best for adding decoration to your paper crafts.

Tape

Sticky tape is perfect for holding your projects together. Double-sided tape works best when you don't want the tape to show.

Foam pads

Sticky foam pads are similar to double-sided tape, but have a foam layer that creates a three-dimensional effect.

Quilling tool

A quilling tool is a small metal or plastic rod with a slit, fixed into a handle. You thread the end of your paper into the slit and turn the tool to make a coil.

poster paint

Scoring tool

A scoring tool has a metal ball fixed to the end of a handle. It can be used to make an indent in thick paper, which makes folding easier. You can use any pointed, blunt object for scoring, e.g. a knitting needle, a slim paintbrush handle or a ballpoint pen that has run out of ink.

glitter glue

PVA glue

TECHNIQUES

When folding card or thicker paper it is best to score the paper first, to make folding easier and more even.

SCORING

1 Place a ruler where you want to make a fold. Run a scoring tool (see page 7) along the edge of the ruler, pressing down hard to leave a mark. It does not matter which side of the paper you score.

You can also use a scoring tool without a ruler to draw curved lines. This will make a gently curved fold (see page 13).

2 The paper or card will fold along the score mark very neatly. Press along the fold with your nail to sharpen it.

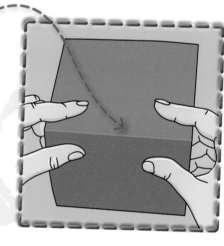

IRIS FOLDING TEMPLATE

For the iris folding technique on page 20 you will need to trace and use this template. The colours are just for guidance.

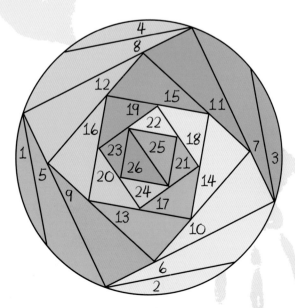

PAPIER MÂCHÉ PASTE

Papier mâché uses newspaper and paste. To make your own paste you'll need plain flour, water, PVA glue, salt, a bowl, a whisk, a teaspoon and a small cup.

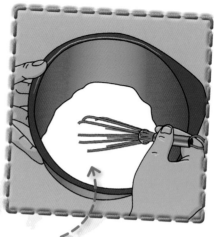

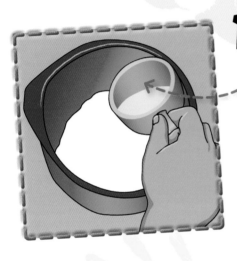

1 Add 1 cup of flour, 1.5 cups of water and 1/3 cup of PVA glue to the bowl. Add a teaspoon of salt to help stop mould from forming.

2 Whisk everything in the bowl until the paste is smooth. Add a little more water if you need to. Cover the bowl until you are ready to use it.

CUTTING AN APERTURE

1 Draw a circle on your card. Fold the card in the centre of the circle, but only crease it gently. Use scissors to make a small cut on the fold.

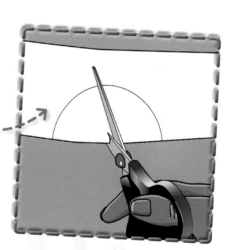

2 Unfold the card. Put the point of the scissors through the hole and cut out the circle.

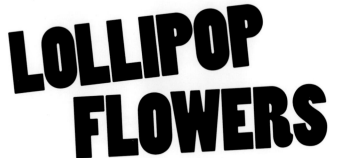

LOLLIPOP FLOWERS

Unwrap these paper flowers to find a surprise – a delicious lollipop!

YOU WILL NEED:

- Tissue paper
- Crêpe paper
- Thin card
- Lollipop
- Glitter glue
- Sticky tape
- All-purpose glue
- Scissors
- Drinking straw

1 Cut a 9 x 9 cm square of tissue paper. Dab dots of glitter glue onto the outside of the square and allow to dry. Wrap the square around the top of a lolly and secure with tape.

2 Cut three 14 x 14 cm squares of tissue paper and two 14 x 14 cm squares of crêpe paper. Fold one square in half diagonally to make a triangle. Fold the triangle in half twice more.

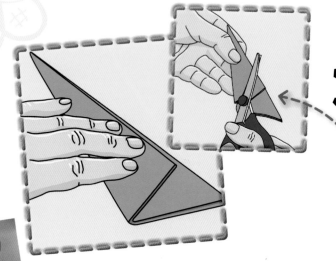

3 Fold in half again to make a narrow triangle. Cut the uneven edge into a curved shape. Cut off the tip of the triangle and then open out to reveal a flower shape. Repeat steps 2 and 3 with all the paper squares.

4 Cut a 9 x 9 cm square of thin card. Follow steps 2 and 3, cutting the tip a little further up to make a larger hole. Reverse every other fold to create a concertina.

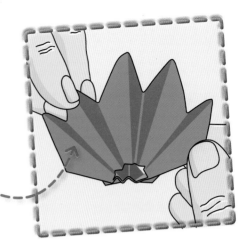

5 Thread all five petal pieces onto the lolly stick, alternating tissue and crêpe paper. Glue the inside of the thin card and stick it to the last petal piece. Add a green straw to make the stem and tape in place.

To make a bee or ladybird, follow step 1 and then cover a small ball of paper with crêpe paper to make a head. Cut card to make wings, and use a pipe cleaner for antennae.

PAPER ROSES

These pretty flowers make a great decoration for any occasion.

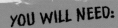
1 Cut a **14 x 14 cm** square of card. Draw a spiral inside the square and then draw a wiggly line along the spiral.

2 Cut along the spiral line and then trim around the wiggly line. This will create the petal shapes.

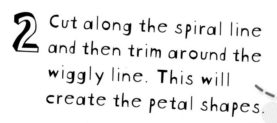

3 Roll the card up tightly, starting at the centre. Hold the rolled card for a few seconds and then let go, so that it opens out. Glue the end of the strip to the side to hold the shape.

4 Use the template to cut a star shape from green card, then fold up each point of the star. Cut out two leaf shapes. Score and fold to create veins (see page 8).

Star template

← 7 cm →

5 Glue the coiled flower to the middle of the star. Glue a bead in the centre, then glue the leaves to the back of the star.

You could also make a smaller version to use as a brooch or tiny versions for earrings.

JAM JAR AQUARIUM

Transform an old jam jar into a colourful nightlight with a layered paper and glue technique called découpage.

1 Tear your tissue paper into small strips. The strips should be roughly 10 x 2 cm but the size and shape can vary.

2 Paint some glue onto your jar. Add a strip of blue paper and paint more glue on top. Continue adding pale blue and turquoise strips until you have covered the jar.

14

3 Add some very thin strips of lime green over the blue and some darker blue strips near the bottom. Leave to dry.

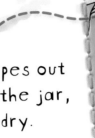

4 Cut some fish and seaweed shapes out of tissue paper. Glue these to the jar, using the paintbrush. Leave to dry.

5 Use glitter glue to add details, such as eyes, fins and bubbles. Leave to dry. Place a battery nightlight inside.

Create your own design. A fairy garden, a sunset or even just a colourful pattern would look fabulous.

FISHY PIÑATA

This traditional Mexican papier mâché toy is filled with sweets and confetti. Take turns to hit it until the sweets fall out!

YOU WILL NEED:

- Newspaper
- Inflated balloon
- Papier mâché paste (see page 9)
- Thick cardboard
- Coloured crêpe paper
- Pin
- Thin, coloured card
- White and green paint
- Paintbrush
- PVA glue
- Scissors
- String

1 Tear a newspaper into squares of about 3 cm. Dip each piece into papier mâché paste and smooth onto the balloon until it is covered. Leave to dry for 4–5 hours. Add three layers, leaving each layer to dry before adding the next.

2 Cut some fins, lips and a tail from thick cardboard. Cover each piece in a layer of papier mâché and leave to dry.

3 Pop the balloon with the pin. Attach the top fin, tail and lips by covering the join with three layers of papier mâché. Let each layer dry before adding the next.

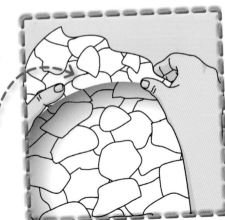

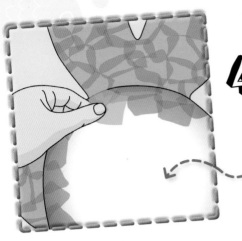

4 Paint the whole fish white and leave to dry. Use watered down PVA glue to apply a layer of crêpe paper over the fins, tail and face of the fish. Leave to dry.

5 Glue on strips of crêpe paper in stripes along the body. Paint the lips. Cut out card circles for the eyes and attach. Glue the side fins into position.

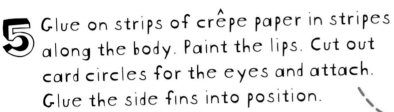

Ask an adult to cut a slit along the side of the top fin. Then fill the piñata with sweets and confetti. Add some string to the top fin and hang the piñata from the ceiling.

MONSTER FOLDING TOY

Make four different monsters with this fun and simple paper toy.

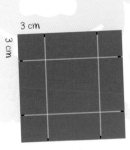

3 cm
3 cm

1 Cut two 12 x 12 cm squares from different colours of thin card. On the back use a pencil to mark eight points, 3 cm away from each corner. Join the opposite points with score lines (see page 8).

2 Turn the two squares over and draw monsters on the fronts. Cut one monster exactly in half horizontally and the other exactly in half vertically.

3 Place the two vertically cut pieces face down side by side. Apply glue to the four corners. Stick the two horizontally cut pieces on top, face up, and allow the glue to dry.

4 Fold the top flap up and the bottom one down to reveal a blank side. Decorate this side with another monster. Paint the outer edge of the centre section to match the top and bottom.

5 Fold again, pulling the centre sections out to the sides. You will notice this side is already partially decorated, so just add the rest of the details.

Experiment with your own designs. You could even try using photos for a personalized version.

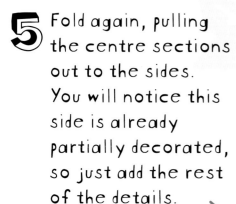

IRIS FOLDED CARD

Make your own greetings cards using a crafting technique called iris folding.

YOU WILL NEED:

- Iris folding template (see page 8)
- 12 x 17.5 cm thin, white card
- 25 x 18 cm thin pink card, folded
- Wrapping paper in four different shades
- Scraps of brown and yellow coloured card
- Glitter glue
- Double-sided sticky tape
- Glue roller or glue stick
- Sticky foam pads
- Sticky tack
- Scissors

7.5 cm

1 Cut a 7.5-cm-wide aperture near the top of the white card (see page 9). Use sticky tack to attach the card face down over the template.

2 Cut four different-coloured strips of paper 2.5 cm wide and 30 cm long. On each strip, fold one long edge over about 5 mm.

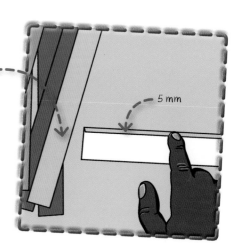

5 mm

3 Take the first strip, face down. Line up the folded edge with section 1 on the template. Cut the strip to fit and glue in place on the edge of the aperture.

20

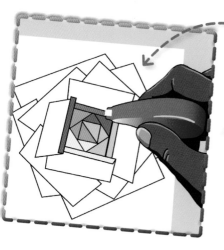

4 Repeat step 3, adding the strips in order and changing the colour each time. Glue each strip to the back of the previous strips, until you reach the centre.

5 Remove from the template and stick the white card to the front of the folded pink card. Cut an ice cream cone and flake out of card. Add glitter glue decoration and leave to dry. Attach to the card using sticky foam pads.

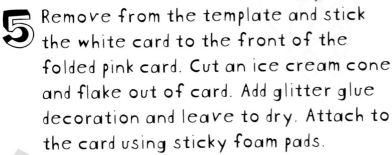

Create a lovely lollipop card instead. Cut a rectangular lolly stick and attach. Stick a small bag over the front of the circle and tie a bow around it.

ZIG-ZAG PHOTO ALBUM

Cut and fold a single sheet of card to make a fun photo album. It makes a great gift!

YOU WILL NEED:

- 30 x 30 cm thin card
- Scraps of thin card
- Patterned paper
- Ribbon
- Stick-on gemstones
- Glue
- Scissors
- Ruler
- Pencil
- Scoring tool (see page 7)

1 Use a pencil and ruler to mark your square of card at 7.5 cm intervals on all four sides. Join the marks to make a grid of 16 squares.

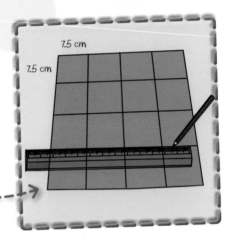

7.5 cm

7.5 cm

2 To create a spiral shape, start at the bottom left corner. Cut three squares to the right, up two squares, left two squares, down one square and then right one square.

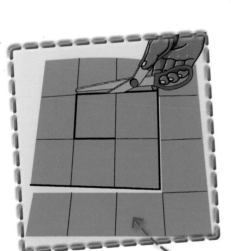

3 Score all the other lines, and fold back and forth on each line to make a concertina-style album.

4 Cut two **40 cm** lengths of ribbon and glue them to the first and last pages. Trim your photos to about **6.5 x 5 cm.** Cut some strips of patterned paper. Glue the paper strips and photos into the album.

5 Cut some flower shapes from thin card. Glue these to the pages and add stick-on gemstones to decorate. Add a title or message if you like.

My birthday

Leave your pages plain and add a pretty front and back cover to make a mini notebook or sticker album.

ORIGAMI BUTTERFLY

Origami is the Japanese art of paper folding. No glue or scissors are needed!

YOU WILL NEED:

- A 15 x 15 cm square of origami paper (or any patterned paper)

1 With the pattern on the outside, fold the paper in half four ways, from side-to-side and diagonally.

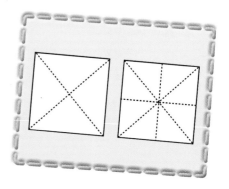

2 Fold the paper in half to make a rectangle. Holding the left side, tuck the right side of the paper towards the centre. Tuck the left side into the centre. You should have a triangle with two flaps on each side.

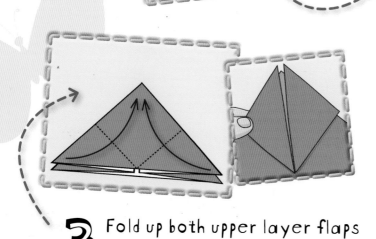

3 Fold up both upper layer flaps to meet the top point.

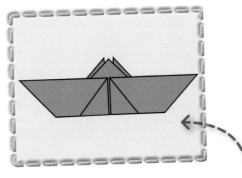

4 Turn it over. Fold all the layers up, leaving a small triangle at the top.

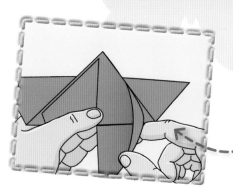

5 Turn it over. Pull the top right flap down gently. The sides will turn up and in. Press them flat. Do the same with the left flap.

6 Turn it over. Fold down the top triangle.

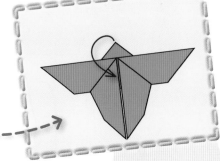

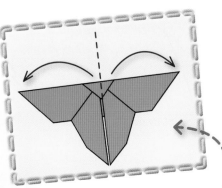

7 Fold in half vertically, folding back so that the wings line up. Keep it folded.

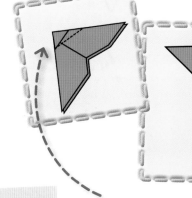

8 Pinch tightly on the small triangle and, while holding, fold back both of the wings. Crease sharply and then allow the wings to fall open.

Make an origami greetings card by attaching your butterfly to a piece of folded card. Add paper clouds and some wire antennae.

KIRIGAMI HANGING STAR

Kirigami is a type of origami that includes paper cutting. Fold, cut and curl to make this star decoration.

YOU WILL NEED:

- Six 10 x 10 cm squares of thick paper or thin card
- String
- Mini stapler or all-purpose glue
- Scissors
- Ruler
- Pencil
- Rubber
- Small hole punch

1 Take one square and fold it in half to make a triangle. Then fold it in half again to make a smaller triangle.

2 Draw a line 0.5 cm from the first folded edge. Cut three slits in the other folded edge, stopping when you get to the line. Try to make the cuts just over 1 cm apart and do not cut right across the paper.

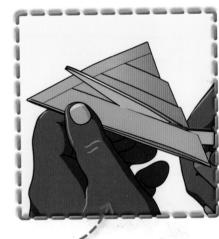

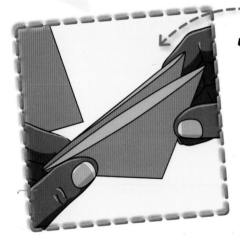

3 Rub out the pencil lines and open out the paper. Roll the central two points to the front until they overlap. Staple or glue them together.

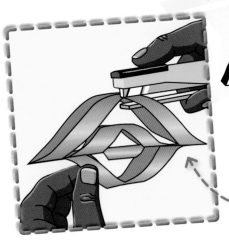

4 Bring the next two points together at the back of the paper and staple. Bring the third set to the front and staple. Staple the last two points at the back. Repeat steps **1** to **4** to make six swirls.

5 Slightly flatten the lower points and staple the swirls together in pairs. Staple two pairs together and then staple or glue the final pair in position. Make a hole in one point and add some string.

Make white stars to look like snowflakes or staple the swirls together to make a chain.

SPANGLY BANGLES

Use papier mâché to create some fun and chunky bangles from newspaper and patterned paper.

1 Cut a strip of card 2.5 x 24 cm. Wrap it around the widest part of your hand to form a circle, remembering it will be a little tighter when the papier mâché is applied. Tape the circle. Cut a second strip and tape it on top to make the bangle stronger.

2 Tear a newspaper into long strips about 2 cm wide. Paste your bangle all over and wrap the strips around the whole bangle. Add 2 or 3 layers before leaving it to dry.

3 Add more layers of papier mâché until you have a chunky bangle. Allow it to dry every **3** or **4** layers. Paint with white paint and leave to dry.

4 Tear some strips from the patterned paper. They should be long enough to go around the outside of the bangle and overlap slightly on the inside. Dip the paper strips in the PVA glue, then smooth them onto the bangle.

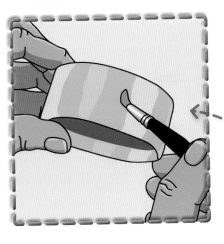

5 Leave the bangle to dry and then add stick-on gemstones. Add another layer of watered-down PVA glue to varnish the bangle. Leave to dry.

Cut thinner strips of card for narrow bangles or cover a cardboard shape in papier mâché to make a matching pendant for a necklace.

QUILLED SHEEP

Use paper strips to create a curly sheep using a technique called quilling. You can roll the strips by hand or use a quilling tool, if you have one.

YOU WILL NEED:

- Black paper strips:
  Legs – 4 strips 1.5 × 30 cm
  Head – 2 strips 0.5 × 30 cm
  Ears – 2 strips 0.5 × 10 cm
- White paper strips:
  Wool and tail –
  9 strips 0.5 × 10 cm
  Body – 1 strip 2 × 30 cm
- White pen
- All-purpose glue
- Sticky tape
- Quilling tool (if you have one)
- Scissors

1 Take the white strip for the body and coil it up tightly. It is easier to do this large roll by hand. Allow the coil to unravel until it's about 2.5 cm across. Glue the end in place.

2 Place the end of a 10 cm white strip into the quilling tool and coil it. Remove from the tool. Allow the coil to unravel slightly and glue the end down. Coil all nine pieces and glue eight together in a circle. The last one is the tail.

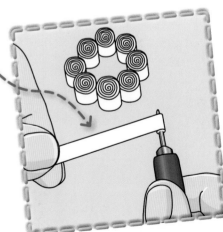

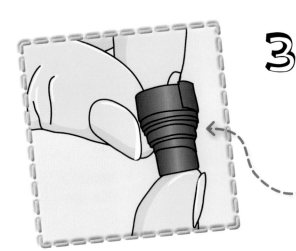

3 Tape the two strips for the head together to make a 60-cm-long strip. Coil it, then allow the roll to unravel slightly and glue the end down. Gently push the centre out to make the head.

4 Coil a leg strip. Hold the roll tight and put a dot of glue on the end to stick it down. Coil the other three legs. Glue the legs together in pairs.

5 Coil the ears and allow the coils to unravel. Glue the ends and pinch them to make raindrop shapes. Glue the head inside the ring of wool coils and add the ears. Glue the head, wool, legs and tail to the body. Draw on eyes.

Use gold and brown strips to make a lion. Add a brown strip to each leg and another strip to make a longer tail. Add a nose and muzzle and two extra coils for a fuller mane.

PAPER CUP OWL

Transform a paper cup and some paper scraps into a cute owl.

YOU WILL NEED:

- Paper cup
- Thin card in various colours and patterns
- All-purpose glue
- Scoring tool (see page 7)
- Ruler
- Pencil
- Scissors
- Paint
- Paintbrush

1 Paint your cup (if you need to). When it is dry, squash the top part of the cup flat and cut off the rim. Shape the top to create two ears.

2 Cut a rough flower shape out of card. Fold it in half and glue it onto the head to hold the two sides together. Squash the ears into shape.

3 Cut an arched piece of card and fold it in half vertically. Cut three angled slits in the fold and open out. Fold the sides into the centre and cut two angled slits in each fold. Open out and glue onto the cup.

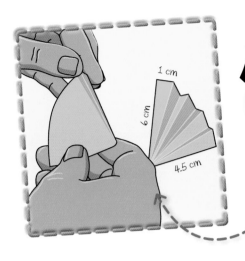

4 Cut two quarter ovals about 6 x 4.5 cm. Mark 1 cm intervals around the curved edge and score lines from the marks to the point. Fold back and forth on each score line to make a concertina. Repeat for the second wing and glue to the sides of the cup.

1 cm
6 cm
4.5 cm

5 To make the eyes, cut out two small, two medium and two large circles. Glue a medium and a small circle on top of each large one, and glue the eyes into position. Cut out a beak and glue in place.

To make a robin, squash the top of the cup. Cut downwards to form a tail, then across the back and up to form the head. Place the eyes and wings on either side of the head.

RECYCLING MATERIALS

Recycling and reusing materials is good for the environment and it saves you pennies. With a little bit of know-how and imagination you can give used or unwanted items a new life. If you turn them into something even better, it's called upcycling.

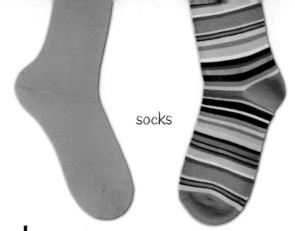

socks

Stuffing

You can reuse stuffing from an old pillow or cushion. If you don't have any, toy stuffing is also available in craft shops.

stuffing

Printed paper

You can find loads of used paper in your home. Used wrapping paper, junk mail, envelopes and unwanted magazines are all perfect for paper projects.

Socks

Who doesn't have a collection of odd socks? Give worn-out or lonely socks a new lease of life with an exciting craft project.

Buttons

Save the buttons from all your old clothes. If you need to buy extra buttons, look in craft shops or search online for really funky ones.

buttons

Beads

You don't always need to buy beads. You can reuse beads from old, unwanted or broken jewellery. Just remember to ask an adult for permission before cutting anything up.

newspapers

envelopes

old jewellery

ties

ribbon
and braid

Ties

Ask your family and friends if they have any old or unwanted ties. If not, you can find cheap, second-hand ties in charity shops.

Greetings cards

Birthday and other greetings cards are far too pretty to throw out, so save them up and recycle them into something fabulous.

greetings cards

Ribbons and braids

You can collect ribbons from gifts and chocolate boxes. You can also buy ribbon and decorative braid from many craft shops.

Stretch elastic

Stretch elastic, also known as jewellery elastic, is available in craft shops. It is best to buy 0.6 mm or 0.8 mm thick elastic so you can thread tiny beads.

stretch
elastic

Brooch backs

To make sturdy brooches, you'll need to sew special brooch backs onto your material. You can buy these in craft shops.

brooch backs

TECHNIQUES
STARTING KNOT

When sewing, it is important to tie a knot in the end of your thread. This will secure the tail of the thread at the back of your fabric.

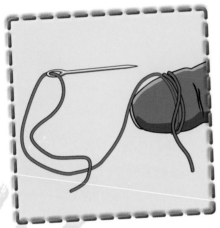

1 Wrap the thread around your index finger.

2 Using your thumb, roll the thread off your finger.

3 Pull the loop towards the end of the thread to make a neat knot.

THREADING

Use a single strand of thread for sewing thin fabrics. For thicker fabrics, or to make your stitches stronger, you can double the thread.

Single threading
Pass the thread through the needle and tie a knot in one end.

Double threading
Pass the thread through the needle. Make sure the needle is in the middle of the thread and knot both ends together.

STITCHING

Running stitch

Sew up and down through the fabric. Make sure the stitches on both the top and the underside are the same size and in a straight line.

Back stitch

Make a running stitch, then come up through the fabric a stitch ahead. Stitch backwards to meet your first running stitch. Repeat in a neat line.

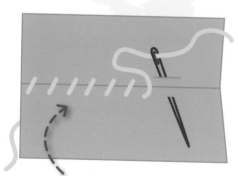

Over stitch

Place the two edges of the fabric you are joining close together. Sew stitches from one piece of fabric to the other to bind them tightly.

Elastic knot

Hold both pieces of elastic together and wrap them around your index finger. Pull through with your other hand. This is similar to tying a balloon.

Finishing knot

To finish sewing, make a small stitch and sew through the loop before pulling it tight. Repeat to make two knots. Cut off the excess thread, leaving a small tail.

BUTTON BRACELET

Make a beautiful bracelet out of buttons. Give it to someone special, or keep it for yourself!

1 Collect 20-40 buttons (depending on their size and who the bracelet is for). Cut 25 cm of elastic (35 cm for an adult). Secure a paper clip 3 cm from one end of the elastic so the buttons won't fall off when you thread them on.

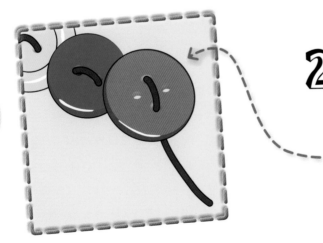

2 Thread the elastic through the front of each button, making the buttons overlap. If a button has two holes, thread the elastic through both. If it has four holes, thread it diagonally through two holes.

3 Wrap the bracelet around your wrist to check the size. A fairly snug fit is best as the buttons will stay flat. Remove the paper clip.

4 Tie the elastic using an elastic knot (see page 37). Cut off the excess elastic, leaving a 0.5 cm tail.

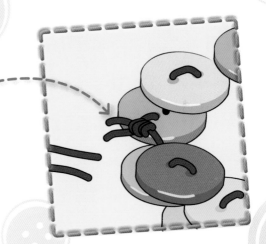

Use your favourite colour combinations or try layering a small button on top of a larger one.

ARMADILLO BROOCH

This quirky armadillo brooch is made from the end of an old tie. Make one to accessorize your clothes, or even a hat or bag.

YOU WILL NEED:

- An old tie
- Paper
- Pencil
- Felt
- Two tiny buttons
- A brooch back
- Needle and thread
- Scissors

1 Cut a 45 cm long piece from the thinner end of a tie. Start rolling it up from the cut edge to make a cone shape. As you roll, use over stitch (see page 37) to sew the fabric along one side. Roll the tie towards the sewing side.

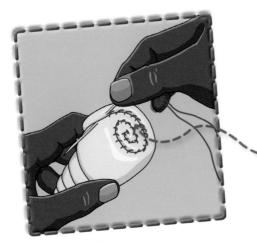

2 When you reach the pointy tip of the tie, fix it in place using a few stitches. You should now have a secure cone shape. This is the armadillo's head.

3 On a piece of paper, draw around the base of the head. Add two pointed ears. Using this as a template, cut out the shape from your felt. Sew the felt to the back of the head.

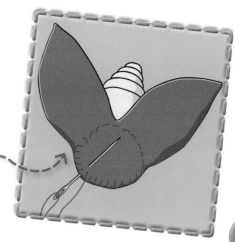

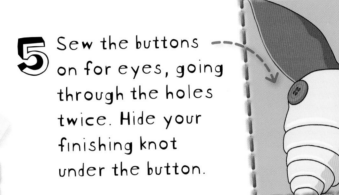

4 Open the brooch back and sew it onto the back of the head. Make sure that it is securely attached.

5 Sew the buttons on for eyes, going through the holes twice. Hide your finishing knot under the button.

Do you want a mouse as well? Make rounded ears and sew on a wool or ribbon tail.

CUPCAKE PINCUSHION

Have you finished with that bottle? Don't throw it away! Wash it out, find two odd socks and make a pincushion.

YOU WILL NEED:

- A used plastic bottle (rinsed clean)
- Two odd socks
- Stuffing
- A bead
- Ribbon or braid
- Needle and thread
- Ruler
- Scissors
- Craft or utility knife

1 Ask an adult to cut the bottom off a plastic bottle, about 5 cm from its base. A craft or utility knife is best for doing this.

2 Measure 9 cm from the top of one sock and cut across. Discard the foot, leaving a tube of material. Pull the tube over the bottle so that the hem fits around the base. Tuck the cut end inside the bottle.

3 Fill the toe part of the second sock with stuffing, until it makes a firm ball. Tie the ball with double thread. Place the ball into the prepared bottle.

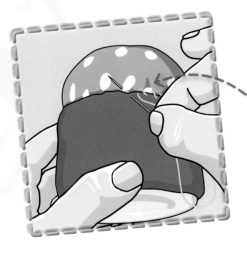

4 Using over stitch (see page 37), sew the two socks together. Sew all the way around.

5 Sew ribbon or braid around the joined socks, using running stitch (see page 37). Top your pincushion with a bead. Now you have a perfect cupcake pincushion with a cherry on top!

You could decorate your pincushion with extra beads or embroidery stitches.

DRAGONFLY PEGS

These colourful dragonfly pegs are a great way to display pictures, photographs or important notes.

1 Spread glue on one side of the peg and stick a piece of paper onto it. Trim the paper so it is the same size as the peg.

head

2 On the plain side of your paper, draw a head, about the size of a ten pence piece. Cut two pieces of paper about 10 x 3 cm and 8 x 3 cm. Fold them in half and draw a wing on each one.

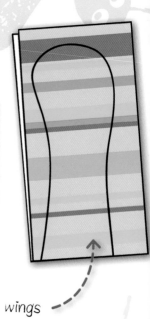

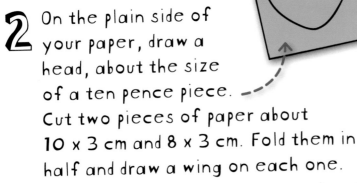

wings

3 Cut out the wings and head, and glue them onto the peg. Cut out a tail shape from the paper and glue it onto the end of the peg.

4 Cut a rectangle from the sweet wrapper and twist it to make the antennae. Shape it into a 'U' and tape it to the back of the head.

5 For the finishing touch, glue on some googly eyes.

Buy a present for Mum

Tidy my bedroom!

Start a new craft project

For extra sparkle, spread glue on the dragonfly's body and sprinkle over lots of coloured glitter.

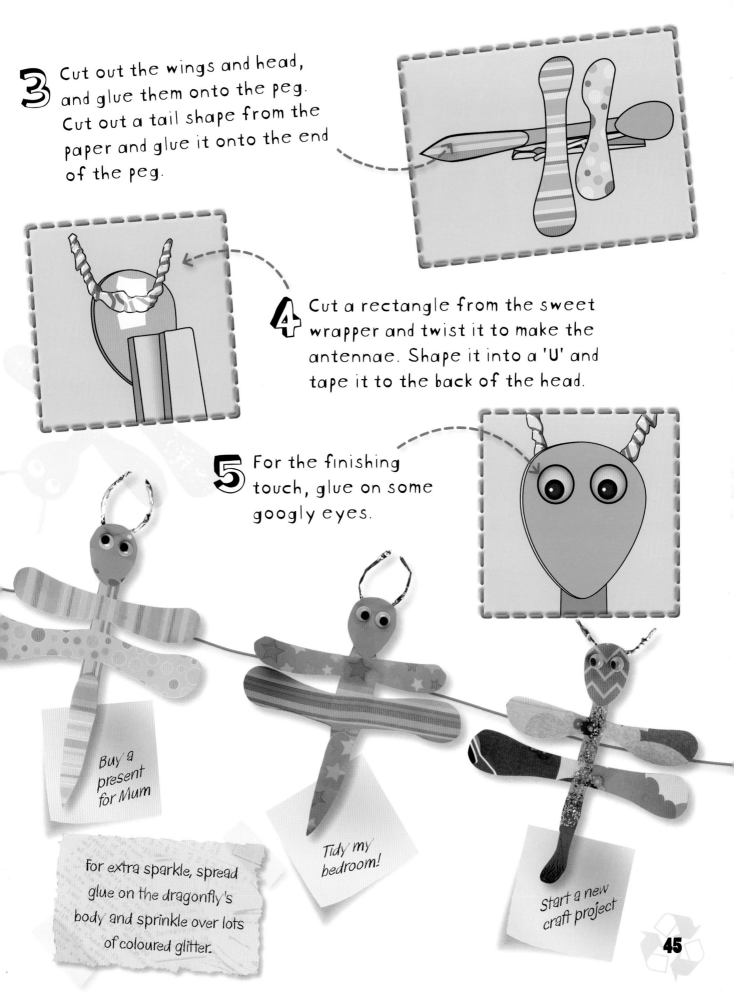

GREETINGS CARD BOX

Recycle a used greetings card to make the perfect little gift box.

YOU WILL NEED:

- A greetings card
- PVA glue and paddle
- Paper clips
- Pencil
- Ruler
- Scissors

1 Cut the card in half. The front will be the top of the box and the back will be the bottom. On the inside of the card back, measure 3 mm from the top and the left. Cut these strips off.

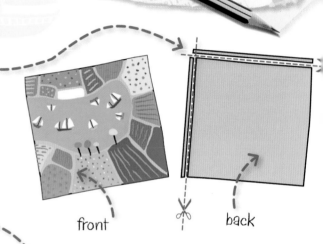

front   back

2 Now follow the same instructions for both pieces of card. On the insides, mark 2 cm margins all the way round.

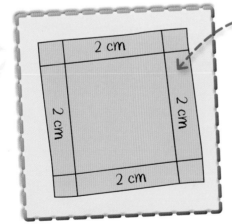

2 cm

2 cm

2 cm

2 cm

3 Hold the ruler firmly on the margin and use the tip of the scissors to score carefully along the lines. Fold the margins up, using the ruler to keep the folds straight.

46

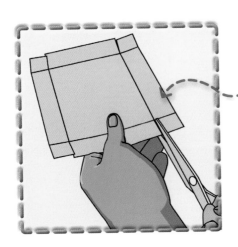

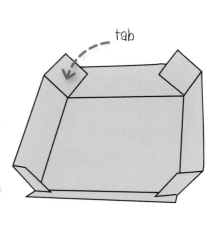

tab

4 Cut two slits at each end of the cards to make four tabs per card.

5 Put glue on the outside of the tabs and fold them in to make a box shape. Secure each corner with a paper clip until the glue is dry.

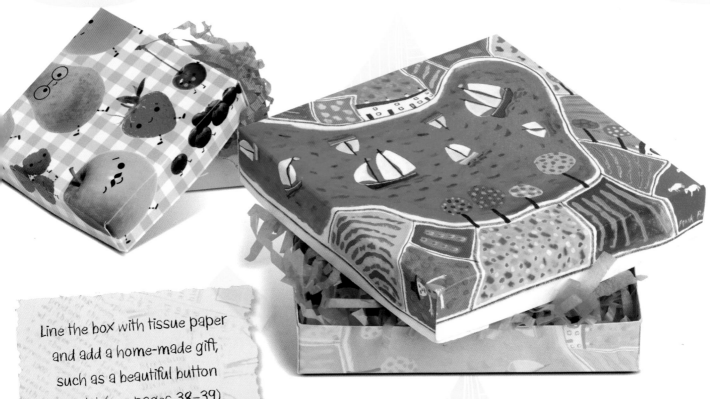

Line the box with tissue paper and add a home-made gift, such as a beautiful button bracelet (see pages 38–39).

JUNK MAIL JEWELLERY

Ask your friends to work out how you made your stylish jewellery. They'll never guess you made the beads from junk mail!

YOU WILL NEED:

- A 210 × 297 mm (A4) piece of junk mail or any used paper
- 8 cocktail sticks
- Glue stick
- Small block of polystyrene or block of modelling clay
- Small beads
- Stretch elastic
- Paper clip
- Clear nail polish or paper varnish
- Ruler
- Pen
- Scissors

1 On the back of the paper, mark 2 cm spaces down one side. On the opposite side, mark 1 cm from the top. Continue with 2 cm marks from this point. Using a ruler, join the marks to make about 20 thin triangles across the page.

1 cm

2 cm

2 cm

2 Cut along the lines you've drawn. You need 6-8 long triangles for one bracelet.

48

3 Starting from the widest end, roll a triangle snugly around the centre of a cocktail stick. Spread glue on the final 10-15 cm of the paper and stick it down firmly. Do the same for each bead.

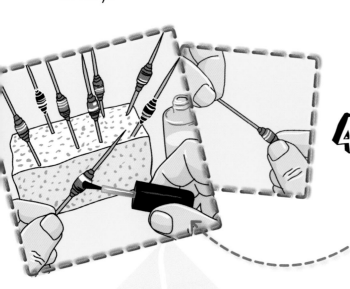

4 Stand the sticks in the polystyrene or clay. Paint each bead with a coat of varnish. Let it dry, then add a second coat. When they are dry, gently twist the beads off the sticks.

5 Cut a piece of elastic slightly bigger than your wrist. Attach a paper clip to one end. Thread on your junk mail beads, adding the smaller beads in between. Tie the bracelet with an elastic knot (see page 37).

How about making a bracelet from an old map?

49

PEG IT PRETTY

Upcycle some old cardboard and paper into a pretty picture display. Then find a good spot on your wall to hang your stylish creation!

YOU WILL NEED:

- Thick cardboard, e.g. an old box
- Ruler
- Glue stick
- 2 large sheets of different coloured paper, e.g. used wrapping paper or leftover wallpaper
- Strong double-sided sticky tape
- 5 flat buttons
- 5 flat wooden pegs
- Ribbon
- Scissors

1 Cut a 30 x 12 cm cardboard rectangle. Glue a slightly larger piece of paper to the cardboard. Tear six 20 cm-long strips of paper and glue them on. Fold and glue any excess paper to the back of the card.

2 Spread glue on one side of a peg and stick a piece of paper to it. Trim the paper so it is the same size as the peg. Do the same to all of the pegs.

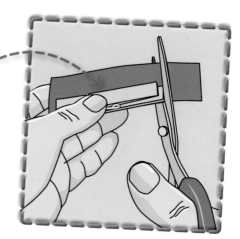

3 Place a piece of double-sided tape on the other side of each peg. Stick the pegs onto the cardboard, between the strips, with the squeezable part at the top.

4 Put double-sided tape on the back of each button. Trim off any excess tape and stick the buttons to the pegs.

5 Cut two loops of ribbon and stick them to the back of the cardboard, at the top. Cut a 28 x 10 cm piece of paper and glue it to the back of the cardboard, over the ribbons.

You could also use your pegs to hold jewellery or notes.

PLASTIC BOTTLE BLOOM

It's so sad when flowers droop and have to be thrown away. But this gorgeous bloom will last forever!

YOU WILL NEED:

- A mini plastic bottle about 10–12 cm high
- Pipe cleaner
- A large button
- A medium-sized button
- Chopstick or similar
- Very small cross-head screwdriver
- Small hammer
- Felt-tip pen
- Scissors

1 Remove any labels from the bottle. Ask an adult to use the hammer and screwdriver to bang a small hole in the lid of the bottle. Screw the lid back on the bottle.

2 Using scissors, carefully cut the bottom off the bottle. Use a felt-tip pen to mark six dots equally spaced around the edge.

3 Use the dots to draw six petal shapes, from the bottom of the bottle to the edge of the lid. Cut out the petals and bend them backwards to open the flower.

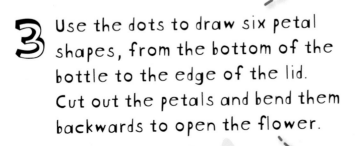

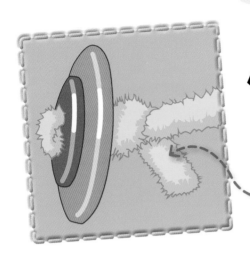

4 Thread the pipe cleaner through both buttons, with the smaller one on top. Make sure that one end of the pipe cleaner is twice as long as the other. Wind the shorter length around the longer end.

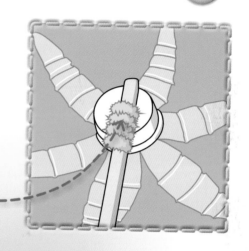

5 Thread the pipe cleaner through the hole in the lid. The button should cover the inside of the lid and the pipe cleaner will be at the back of the flower. Wind the pipe cleaner around a chopstick to make a stem.

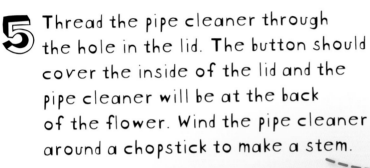

Make a daisy-like flower by cutting shorter petals with rounded ends.

SOCK MONSTER

Collect all your old or odd socks and make a sock monster.

YOU WILL NEED:

- A complete sock
- Scraps from two or more other odd socks
- Needle and thread
- Buttons
- Stuffing
- Scissors

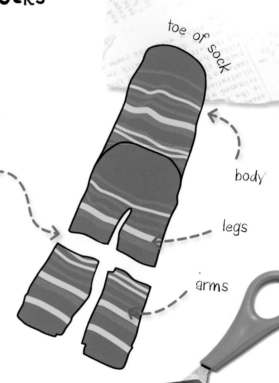

toe of sock

body

legs

arms

1 Turn the complete sock inside out. Lay it flat, with the heel on top. From the open end, cut through the middle of the sock, almost to the heel. These are the legs. Cut across the legs, about half-way up, to make two arms.

2 Sew up the end and side of each leg, using back stitch (see page 37). Leave a gap of about 3 cm between the legs for stuffing. Sew the arms using back stitch, leaving one short side open for stuffing.

3 Turn all the sock parts the right side out. Fill the sock with stuffing, including the legs and arms. Sew the gaps using over stitch (see page 37). Sew the arms to the body with over stitch.

4 Sew buttons on for the eyes. For the mouth, cut the stretchy cuff off the top of a sock and sew it onto the monster with over stitch.

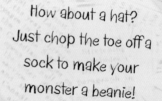

How about a hat? Just chop the toe off a sock to make your monster a beanie!

5 To make the hair, cut eight 1-cm-wide strips of varying lengths from your sock scraps. Sew them to the monster's head with running stitch (see page 37).

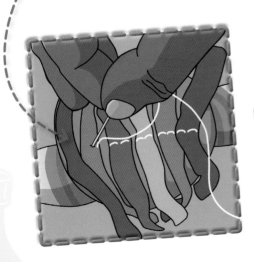

TOPSY-TURVY POT

Upcycle old paper into a stylish topsy-turvy pot! It looks cool and is great for storing all your crafty bits and bobs.

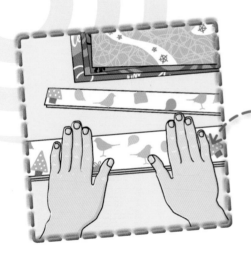

1 Cut twenty 15 x 30 cm pieces of paper. Fold each piece in half three times, lengthways. Secure both ends of each strip with a small piece of tape. You will have 20 strips which are about 2 x 30 cm long.

2 Wind a strip into a tight spiral and fix the end down with a piece of sticky tape.

3 Add a second strip to the spiral with some sticky tape. Wind it around the first spiral and stick the end down with tape. You will now have a bigger spiral. Continue adding strips until all 20 are attached.

4 Slowly and gently pull the circles up to make a bowl shape. The bowl can be straight or crooked, whichever you prefer. Be careful not to push too far, or your bowl may unwind!

5 Carefully paint the pot inside and out with PVA glue to help it hold its shape. Allow it to dry and then paint it twice more.

To add handles, glue or tape two small spirals on opposite sides of the pot and allow them to dry. Then add two mini spirals. Add three layers of PVA glue.

YO-YO BROOCH

Jazz up an old piece of clothing by turning it into a stylish yo-yo brooch.

YOU WILL NEED:

- Cotton, linen or polyester fabric from worn-out clothes
- Pen
- Soup or dessert bowl
- Scissors
- Needle and thread
- Button
- Brooch back

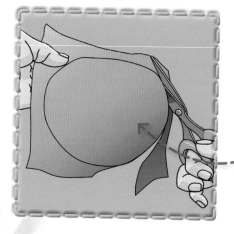

1 Use the bowl to trace a circle on the back of your fabric. Cut out the circle.

2 Cut 70 cm of thread and double thread the needle (see page 36). Sew running stitch (see page 37) around the front of the fabric, about 0.5 cm from the edge.

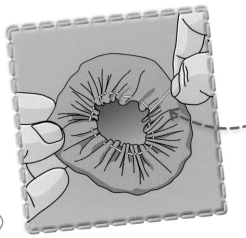

3 Without cutting the thread, gently pull it to gather the material together. Flatten the material. Make a stitch and knot where the pleats meet in the centre. Don't cut off the thread yet.

4 Using the same thread, sew the button over the pleat. Make sure that your stitches go right through to the back of the fabric.

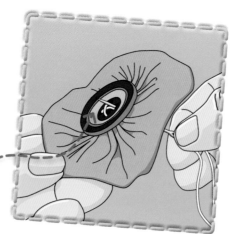

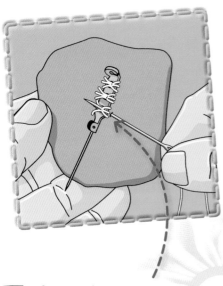

5 Sew the brooch back to the fabric, making 3-4 stitches through each hole to secure it.

For a layered brooch, make a smaller yo-yo brooch by drawing around a mug. Add a fabric circle between the two yo-yos and sew all three layers together.

EASY-PEASY GIFT BOW

Make your presents look fabulous by adding a home-made gift bow.

YOU WILL NEED:

- A sheet of used paper, such as a magazine
- String or strong yarn
- Sticky tape
- Glue stick
- Ruler
- Pen
- One large and one medium-sized button
- Scissors

1 Cut the paper to 30 x 10 cm. Measure 1 cm from the narrowest edge of the paper and draw a line. Fold the paper along this line.

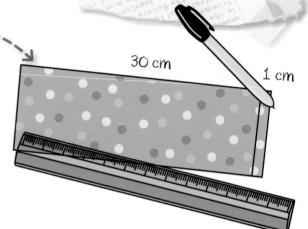

30 cm   1 cm

2 Fold the paper alternately forwards and backwards 1 cm to create a concertina. Cut both ends at an angle and fold the concertina in the middle.

3 Place the medium button on top of the large one and thread onto the string. Tie the string around the middle of the concertina, knotting it at the back.

60

4 Spread glue along half of one side of the paper. Join the halves together, holding firmly to make them stick. Do the same with the other side to make a circle.

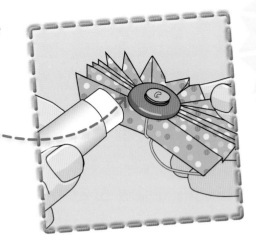

5 Add a strip of sticky tape to the back of the circle, where the paper joins. This will strengthen it. Tie your bow to a gift using the string.

Make the gift bow into a paper flower by tying the string to a chopstick, dowel rod or coffee stirrer.

JEWELLERY MATERIALS

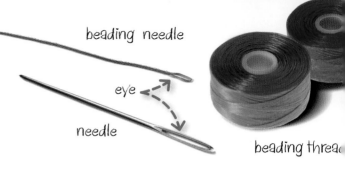

beading needle

eye

needle

beading thread

Beads, beading thread, clasps, chain and wire are sold in craft shops, department stores and online. You can also visit speciality bead shops for a huge range of colours and styles.

Découpage glue

You can purchase pre-made découpage glue. You can also make your own by mixing two parts of PVA glue to one part water.

seed beads

Seed beads

These small beads come in varying sizes – the higher the number, the smaller the bead. You can use any size for the projects in this book, but larger sizes are easier to work with. Make sure that your needle has a small enough eye for the beads to slide over.

Beading thread and beading elastic

Beading thread is stronger than ordinary thread. Beading elastic is a thin stretchy cord.

Beading needle

Beading needles are made of a strong, flexible wire so that beads can pass easily over the eye. You can use a regular needle if the eye is small enough for the beads to pass over.

Jump ring

A jump ring is a metal loop that you can open to put on beads or charms.

jump rings

skein of embroidery thread

crochet
hooks

Cord

There are many types of cord available. You can purchase leather, or a less expensive cord that looks like leather, in a variety of colours.

ball chain

Ball chain

This inexpensive chain is made up of little metal balls. It is easy to cut to the correct length with scissors or nail clippers and is sold with clasps. Ball chains also come in a variety of colours.

Embroidery thread

There are two kinds of embroidery thread, one with strands that you can separate, and one that you can't separate. Either kind is fine for friendship bracelets, but always use the same kind in any single bracelet.

Glue

Any kind of glue that dries clear (PVA is a good choice) can be used to dab onto knots in thread to stop them from unravelling.

Crochet hook

Crochet hooks come in different sizes. It is important to use the hook size given in the project instructions if you can, but it is OK to substitute a hook that is one size above or below.

Jewellery clasps

You will find a wide variety of clasps wherever jewellery supplies are sold. Choose one that will look good with your project and is easy to open and close.

jewellery clasps

Wire

Wire comes in different gauges. The higher the number of the gauge, the thinner the wire, and the more flexible it is.

wire

PVA glue

TECHNIQUES

DÉCOUPAGE

Découpage is the art of gluing bits of paper or fabric onto an object. You can use this technique to make beads (see pages 72-73) or other art and craft projects.

CROCHET TIPS

Here are some tips to help you with the projects on pages 82-85. It is a good idea to practise your crochet technique before you begin these crafts.

Slip Knot

1 Crocheting starts with a slip knot. Make a loop near the end of the thread.

2 Make another loop in the tail end of the wool and push it through the first loop. Pull tight.

Keeping tension in the wool

Hold the crochet hook in your writing hand. Hold the wool in your other hand and use your index finger to keep the wool tight.

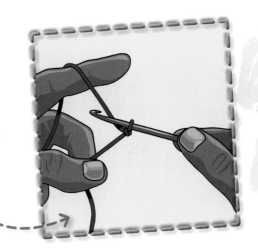

Creating new rows

To create the first row, see page 82 for instructions.

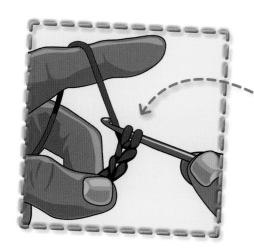

1 To start the second row, stick the crochet hook in the second loop from the hook, hook the wool and bring it through just the first loop. You will now have two loops on the crochet hook.

2 Hook the wool again and bring it through both loops. Repeat the process to the end of the chain.

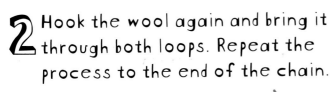

3 For the third row, insert the hook through the top two loops, then work as steps 1 and 2, pulling the wool through one and then both loops. Use this method to crochet as many rows as you want.

FRIENDSHIP BRACELET

Friendship bracelets are fun to make and to share. This diagonal stripe pattern is a classic.

YOU WILL NEED:

- Three colours of embroidery thread
- Scissors
- Sticky tape

1 Cut two 30 cm pieces of each colour of embroidery thread. Gather the six strands together and tie a knot at the top, leaving a 10 cm tail. Tape the thread down, just above the knot.

2 Sort the strands by colour. Take the first strand and loop it over the second strand, so it looks like a '4'. Take the first strand underneath the second strand and through the loop.

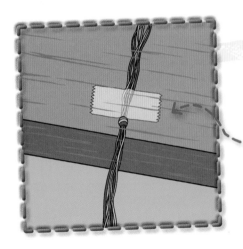

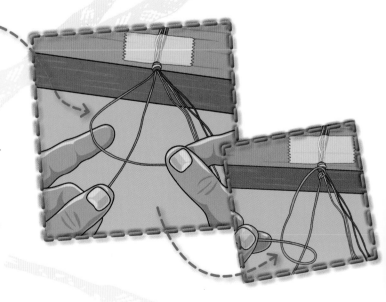

3 You should now have a knot. Hold the second strand straight and taut while you tighten the knot. Repeat step 2 to make a second knot on the same strand. You have now made a double knot.

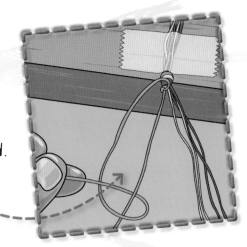

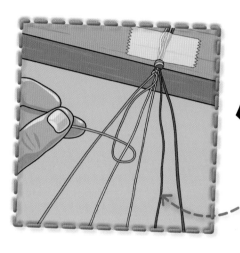

4 With the same thread, double knot around each of the remaining strands, just as you did in steps 2 and 3. Go from left to right, holding the strands straight and tight as you knot.

5 You should now have a different thread on the far left. Repeat steps 2, 3 and 4. Keep going until the bracelet is as long as you want. Tie a knot with all the strands at the end of the bracelet.

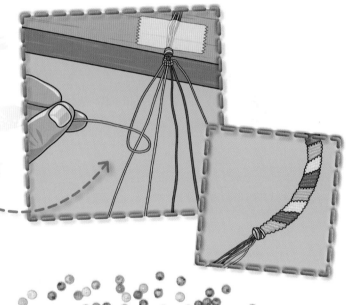

Give a friendship bracelet to each of your best friends to show how much you care.

WRAP FRIENDSHIP BRACELET

This colourful knotted bracelet looks great wrapped around your wrist several times.

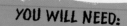

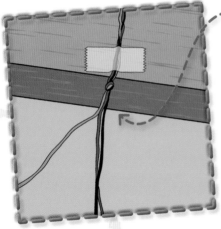

1 Tie a knot at the top of the three lengths of thread, leaving 10 cm of thread above the knot. Tape the thread down, just above the knot. Pull one strand to the left of the other two.

2 Take the left strand and loop it over the other strands, so it looks like a '4'. Take the strand underneath the others and through the loop. This will form a knot.

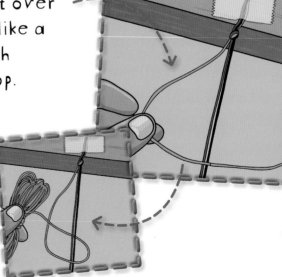

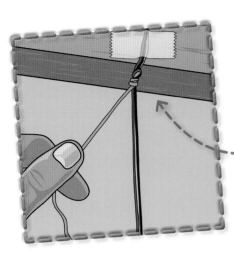

 Hold the two other strands straight and tighten the knot. Repeat step 2 until you want to change colours.

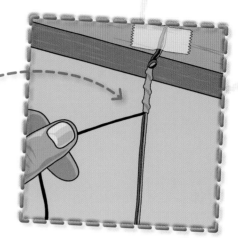

4 To change colours, pull a different coloured strand out to the left. Repeat steps 2 and 3.

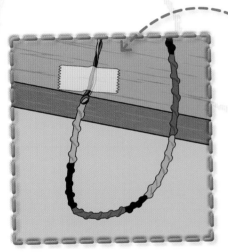

5 When the bracelet is long enough, tie a knot at the end. Trim the tails at both ends so they are just long enough to tie the bracelet together.

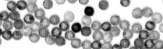

Experiment with different colours. Try four or five colours when you have mastered three.

FRIENDSHIP BEADS

You can string these colourful beads together to make bracelets or necklaces, or swap them with your friends.

1 Cut a piece of thread about 1 m long. Thread it through the bead and tie a knot around the bead. Trim the short end of the thread.

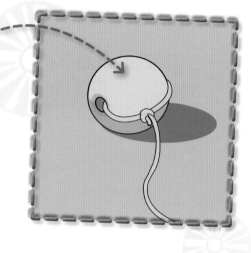

2 Put a dab of glue on the knot. Turn the thread so the knot is inside the bead. Leave to dry.

3 Using the needle, take the thread around the bead and through the hole. Pull the thread tight.

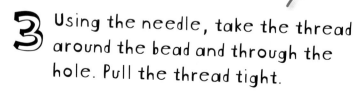

4 Repeat step 3 until the bead is covered. Pull the thread tight every time.

5 Knot the thread at the top of the bead and pull tight. Trim the thread and put a dab of glue on the knot. Use the needle to push the knot inside the bead.

Use the same method if you want to layer another colour on top. To make a striped bead, thread two colours of thread onto the same needle and follow the steps.

DÉCOUPAGE NECKLACE

This is a fun way to turn scraps of fabric into a wearable work of art.

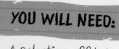

YOU WILL NEED:

- A selection of fabric scraps
- 10 large wooden beads
- Scissors
- Découpage glue (see page 62)
- Paintbrush
- Skewer
- Bowl

1 Cut a scrap of fabric that fits halfway around a bead and then cut it into smaller strips. Thread a bead onto a skewer.

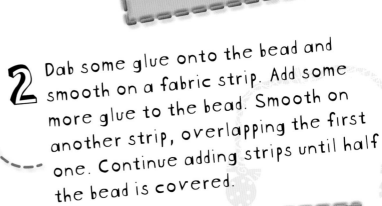

2 Dab some glue onto the bead and smooth on a fabric strip. Add some more glue to the bead. Smooth on another strip, overlapping the first one. Continue adding strips until half the bead is covered.

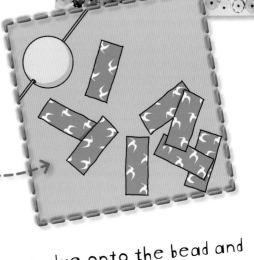

3 Paint glue over the covered part of the bead and rest the skewer over a bowl to let the bead dry. Repeat step 2 to cover the second half of the bead. Follow steps 1, 2 and 3 to cover ten beads. Leave the beads to dry.

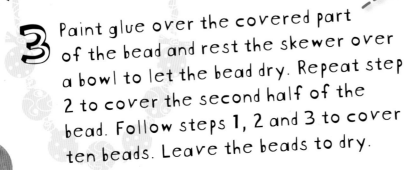

4 Cut a strip of fabric 1 cm wide and 1 m long. Cut one end at an angle. Thread on the beads, knotting the fabric in between each bead.

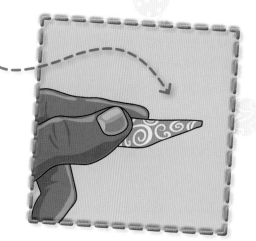

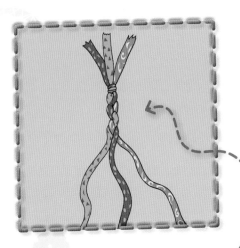

5 Cut six strips of fabric about 40 cm long. Make two plaits and knot the ends. Tie them to the ends of the necklace and knot together.

If you make a few extra beads, you can create a matching bracelet. Instead of knotting between each découpage bead, try adding a smaller wooden bead.

WOVEN BEAD BRACELET

Turn an ordinary hair comb into a loom to make these woven bracelets. You can use different colour combinations to make unique designs.

YOU WILL NEED:

- Three 65 cm long pieces of embroidery thread
- One 1 m piece of beading thread
- Beading needle
- Seed beads
- Comb
- Sticky tape
- Scissors

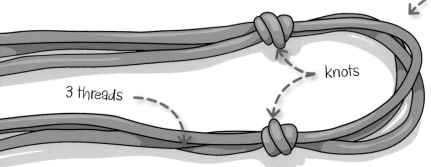

3 threads

knots

1 Hold the three pieces of embroidery thread together. Find the centre point of the thread and tie a knot on each side, 2 cm from the centre.

2 Tape the comb to the edge of a table with the teeth sticking up. Place the knots behind the comb and tape down the thread loop. Separate the six pieces of thread and slip them through the teeth of the comb.

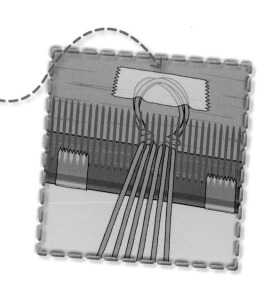

3 Thread the beading thread onto the needle and tie a knot at the end. Take the needle through the left knot. Thread five seed beads onto the needle.

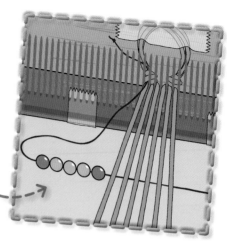

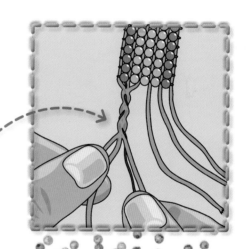

4 Pass the needle underneath the strands of thread. Push the beads up between the strands with your finger. Pass the needle over the top of the strands and through the beads in the opposite direction.

5 Repeat steps 3 and 4 until the bracelet is the desired length (about **45 rows**). Make the strands into two plaits. Plait the extra beading thread with one of the strands and then tie a knot at the end of each plait. Trim the ends.

Weave double the number of rows to make a dramatic choker-style necklace.

PRETTY PIN BROOCH

This brooch is simple yet stylish. Wear one on its own or create a few to wear together.

YOU WILL NEED:

- Safety pin
- 24 or 28 gauge wire
- About 20 seed beads and some larger beads
- Large jump ring
- Wire clippers or fingernail clippers

1 Cut a piece of wire about 20 cm long. Twist one end of the wire around the bottom of the safety pin two or three times.

2 Thread three or four seed beads onto the wire. On the side of the pin that does not open, wind the wire around twice to keep the beads in place.

3 Continue threading more beads, adding some larger beads as well. Wind the wire around the pin after every three or four beads.

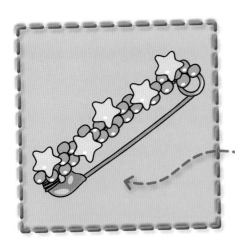

4 When you get to the end of the pin, wind the wire around it three times to secure it. Cut the wire close to the pin.

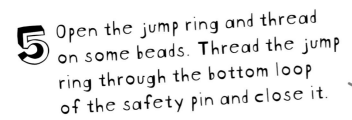

5 Open the jump ring and thread on some beads. Thread the jump ring through the bottom loop of the safety pin and close it.

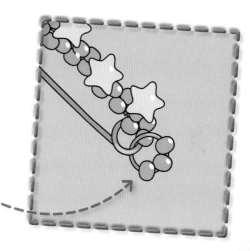

Experiment with different coloured beads to match your favourite outfits. These brooches make great gifts, too!

FLOWER POWER HAIRBAND

You'll never have another bad hair day with this colourful hair accessory.

YOU WILL NEED:

- Felt
- Pen
- Ruler
- Scissors
- Needle
- Thread
- Cotton wool ball
- Bead
- Hairband

1 Draw a circle on the felt about 6 cm wide and cut it out. Cut four 1.5 cm slits into the circle, equal distances apart.

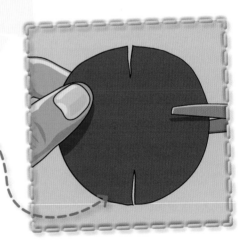

2 Cut four more slits between the first four to make eight equal-sized petals. Cut each petal so it forms a half circle on one side.

3 Thread the needle and knot the end. Take the needle through the tip of each petal, coming from the inside of the flower each time.

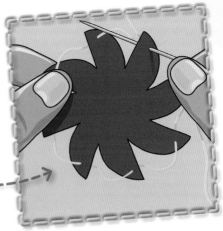

4 Go through the first petal again to complete the circle. Put a cotton wool ball in the centre of the flower. Pull the thread tight so the circle is closed. Make a stitch and knot the thread.

5 Thread on a bead and sew it onto the fabric. Take the needle through to the back of the flower and sew on a hairband. Tie a knot and trim the thread.

There are lots of ways to use these felt flowers. You could make a brooch or sew a flower onto the headband from page 82.

TWISTED BRACELET

Turn a simple ball chain into something special with some cord and embroidery thread. Two or three of these bracelets look great on your wrist.

YOU WILL NEED:

- Ball chain with clasp
- Scissors
- Leather or cotton cord
- Embroidery thread
- Glue

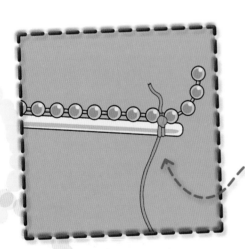

1 Take the end of the chain without the clasp and cut it to fit your wrist. Cut the cord about 2 cm shorter than the chain and cut the embroidery thread to four times the length of the cord. Use the thread to tie the chain and the cord together, leaving two or three chain links at the end.

2 Put a dab of glue on the knot. Wrap the thread tightly around the cord, chain and tail of the thread.

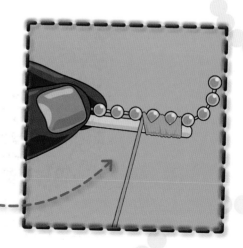

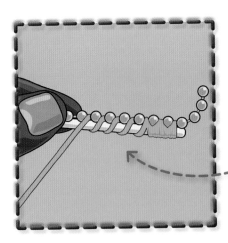

3 Wrap the thread around the chain and cord, going in between each link of the chain. As you do this, the chain will naturally twist around the cord.

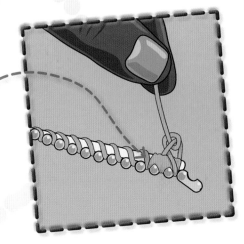

4 When you get to the clasp end, tie the thread in a knot. Wrap the thread around a few times to secure everything in place.

5 Tie another knot with the thread. Trim the end of the thread and put a dab of glue on the knot.

You can use the same method to make a necklace. Tape one end of the chain to a table to make wrapping the longer length easier.

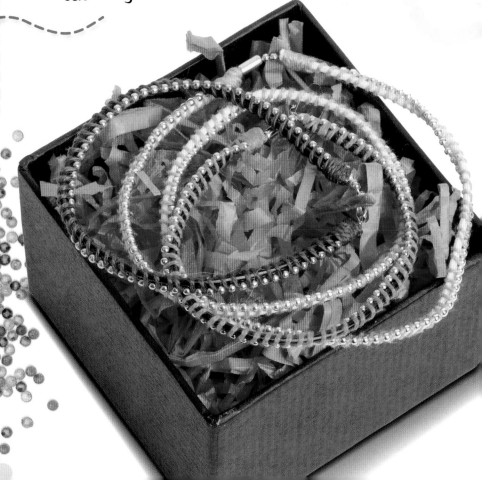

CROCHET HEADBAND

Crochet these thick or thin, in any colour. Tie one around your head for a hippy chick look.

YOU WILL NEED:

- Wool
- Size 4 mm crochet hook (UK size 8, US size 6)
- Scissors

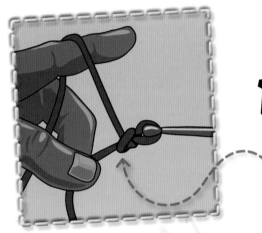

1 Make a slip knot (see page 64) in the wool, leaving a 15 cm tail. Insert the crochet hook and tighten the knot until it is slightly loose around the hook. Keeping tension (see page 65), hook the wool and bring it through the loop.

2 You will now have a new loop on the crochet hook. Repeat step 1 until the row of stitches is almost long enough to fit around your head.

3 Start a new row (see steps 1 and 2 on page 65). Repeat to the end of the chain.

4 Crochet as many rows as you need (see page 65). Cut the wool, leaving a 15 cm tail. Remove the crochet hook and pull the wool through the remaining loop.

5 Trim the wool on both ends of the headband so they are even. Use the wool ends to tie the headband in place.

Use multi-coloured wool for a rainbow effect or add a felt flower from page 78.

STRETCHY RINGS

Once you master a single crochet stitch, you'll be hooked on making these stretchy, colourful rings.

1 Make a slip knot in the cord (see page 64), leaving a 4 cm tail. Insert the crochet hook and tighten the knot until it is only slightly loose. Keeping tension on the elastic cord (see page 65), hook the cord and bring it through the loop.

2 You will now have a new loop on the crochet hook. Repeat step 1 until the row of stitches is long enough to go around your finger.

3 Stick the crochet hook through the first loop. Hook the cord and bring it through both loops to make a circle.

4 Stick the crochet hook in the second loop and bring it through just the first loop (you will now have two loops on the hook). Hook the cord again and bring it through both loops. Repeat all the way around the ring. Add at least 2 rows.

5 After the last stitch, cut the cord, leaving a **4 cm** tail. Pull it through the loop on your crochet hook. Remove the hook and tie the two ends together on the inside of the ring. Put a dab of glue on the knot and trim the ends.

You can choose how thick or thin your ring is by adding as many rows as you want.

TRIPLE STRAND BRACELET

You'll want to wear this pretty bracelet every day. Why not make one to match all your favourite outfits?

YOU WILL NEED:

- Beading thread
- Beading needle
- A clasp
- Seed beads
- Other small beads
- Sticky tape
- Glue
- Scissors

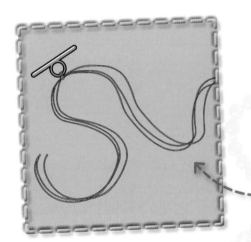

1 Cut three 50 cm pieces of thread. Hold the strands together and thread them through one end of the clasp. Leave a 12 cm tail and knot the thread around the clasp.

2 Thread the beading needle onto one of the long strands of thread. Use the needle to thread on seed beads until the bracelet is as long as you want. Take off the needle and put a piece of tape around the thread to hold the beads in place.

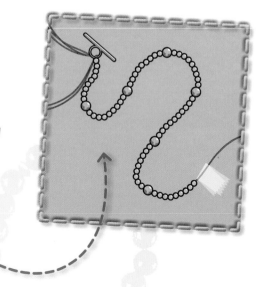

3 Repeat step 2 with the other two strands, making sure that they are all the same length. Take the tape off the strands and gather them together.

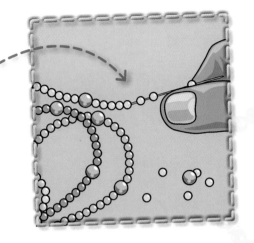

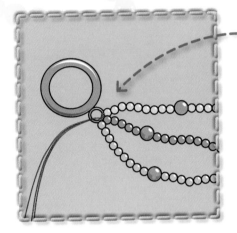

4 Thread all three strands onto the needle. Take the needle through the other end of the clasp twice and pull it tight.

5 Thread the needle through three seed beads on one strand. Tie a knot between the beads. Dab some glue on the knot and trim the ends of the thread. Repeat on the other end of the bracelet.

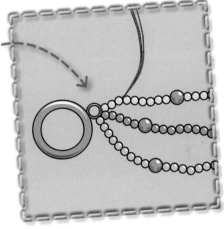

Try mixing in silver beads with the seed beads for extra sparkle.

DAISY CHAIN NECKLACE

Use seed beads to make a daisy chain you can keep forever.

YOU WILL NEED:

- Seed beads in three colours
- A clasp
- Beading thread
- Beading needle
- Scissors
- Glue

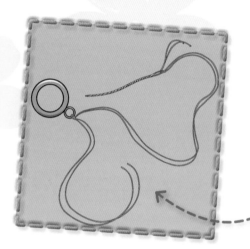

1 Cut a piece of beading thread four times the length you want your necklace to be. Double-thread the needle and pull it to the centre of the thread. Tie the two ends of the thread around one side of the clasp, leaving a **10 cm** tail.

2 String ten seed beads onto the thread. Then string six more beads in the colour you want your flower to be. Bring the needle back up through the first flower bead. Pull the thread to make a circle.

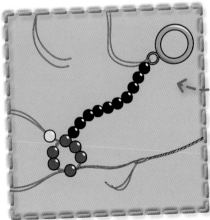

3 String on one bead in another colour to make the centre of the flower. Take the needle through the fourth flower bead. Pull tight.

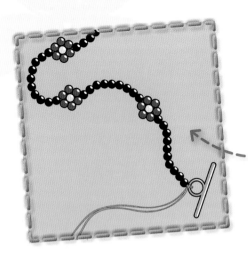

4 Repeat steps 2 and 3 until your necklace is the desired length. Take the needle through the other side of the clasp twice. Pull tight.

5 Take the needle through three beads. Tie a knot between the beads. Put a dab of glue on the knot and trim the ends of the thread. Repeat on the other end of the necklace.

Create a shorter chain to to make a daisy chain bracelet.

yarn

KNITTING MATERIALS

darning needle

Yarn
Commonly spun from wool or acrylic fibres, yarn comes in many colours and thicknesses. Most projects are made in standard double knitting (DK) yarn or in thicker, chunky yarn.

Knitting needles
Different sizes, or thicknesses, of needles are used for different types of yarn. In this book you will be using 3.25 mm, 4 mm and 6.5 mm needles.

Darning needle
A thick needle with a large eye and blunt point, used for sewing yarn.

Sewing needle and thread
A thin needle and fine thread, best for sewing on buttons and fasteners.

Felt
This thick cloth is great for adding details to knitted projects.

Air erasable fabric pen
The ink in this pen becomes invisible over 24 hours so it is great for marking on felt. You could also use tailor's chalk.

Crochet hook
A short, hooked tool, useful for hooking yarn through gaps in knitting.

knitting needles

TECHNIQUES

Garter stitch
Knit every row (see page 92). Both sides will look the same.

Stocking stitch
Knit a row, then purl a row (see page 92). The front will have rows of 'v' stitches, the back will look like garter stitch.

Changing yarn colour
On a new row, tie the tail of the new yarn to the end of the old yarn and start knitting with the new colour.

Darning in loose ends
Sew in loose yarn by taking the needle through a few stitches at the back of the fabric.

CASTING ON

1 Make a loop of yarn. Pull another loop through it and place it onto a needle. Pull tighter.

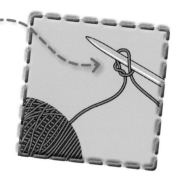

2 Insert the tip of the right needle through the front of the loop and under the needle.

3 Wind the yarn under and over the point of the right needle.

4 Use the right needle to draw the yarn through the stitch and create a loop.

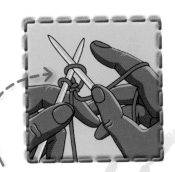

5 Insert the left needle into the back of the loop to make a second stitch.

6 Repeat steps 2 to 5 until you have the required number of stitches.

CASTING OFF

1 Knit two stitches. Insert the left needle into the first stitch knitted. Lift it and pull it over the second stitch.

2 Knit the next stitch. Lift the first stitch over the second. Repeat this until one stitch is left on your right needle. Cut the yarn and pull the tail through the last stitch.

KNIT STITCH

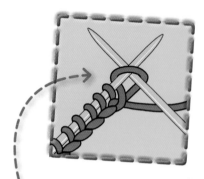

1 Insert the point of the right needle into the front of the first stitch from front to back.

2 Wind the yarn under and over the point of the right needle.

3 Use the right needle to pull the yarn through the stitch to create a loop. Slip the stitch off the left needle.

PURL STITCH

1 Hold the needle with stitches in your left hand. Insert the point of your right needle into the first stitch, from back to front.

KNIT 2 TOGETHER
This is just like a knit stitch. Insert your right needle into two stitches. Wrap the yarn around the needle as normal, pull it through, then slip both stitches off your left needle.

2 Wind the yarn around the right needle tip from right to left.

3 Use your right needle to pull the yarn back through the stitch to create a loop.

4 Slip the stitch off the left needle. You now have one purl stitch made on your right needle.

SEWING TECHNIQUES

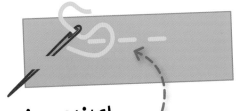

Running stitch

Sew up and down through the fabric. Make sure the stitches on both the topside and underside are the same size and in a straight line.

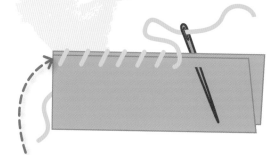

Over stitch

Place the two edges of the fabric you are joining close together. Sew stitches from one piece of fabric to the other to bind them tightly.

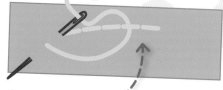

Back stitch

Make a running stitch, then come up through the fabric a stitch ahead. Stitch backwards to meet your first running stitch. Repeat in a neat line.

KNITTING A TENSION SQUARE

Some patterns in this book suggest you knit a tension square first. This helps you to check that your knitting will come out at the right size.

Knit a square slightly larger than 10 x 10 cm. Follow the tension square pattern, then count how many 'v' stitches there are horizontally and how many 'v' rows there are vertically in a 10 x 10 cm area. This will give you your 'tension gauge', e.g. 24 stitches x 30 rows.

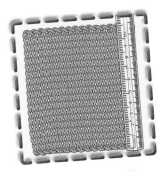
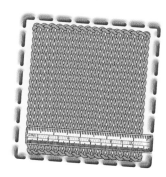

If you have more stitches and rows in your square than there are in the 'pattern gauge', change to larger needles. If you have fewer stitches and rows change to smaller needles.

FLOWER PURSE

Use star stitch to decorate this handy knitted purse.

YOU WILL NEED:

- Red DK yarn
- A small quantity of yellow DK yarn
- A small quantity of orange DK yarn
- 4 mm knitting needles
- 1 large and 3 small buttons
- Yellow sewing thread
- Red sewing thread
- 15 mm snap fastener
- Darning needle
- Sewing needle
- Round end pins
- Tape measure
- Scissors

START HERE

Knitting pattern

FINISHED ITEM LAID FLAT MEASURES: 10 × 8 cm

BEGIN: Cast on 24 stitches in red yarn.

NEXT: Knit every row until your work measures 20 cm.

END: Cast off.

STAR STITCH

Pull your needle up through at point 1 and re-insert your needle at point 2. Pull up your needle at point 3 and re-insert at point 4, and so on.

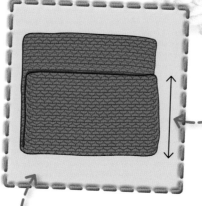

8.5 cm

1 Measure 8.5 cm from the cast off edge and fold the fabric over to make the body of the purse.

2 Fold over the top flap. Use a darning needle and the yellow yarn to sew the large button in the centre.

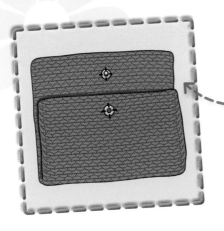

3 Using the sewing thread, sew the top of the snap fastener onto the underside of the flap, under the button. Sew the bottom of the snap fastener onto the body of the purse so that it lines up with the top fastener.

4 Use double-threaded yarn and star stitch to sew one large star and two smaller ones onto the front of the purse. Sew the small buttons onto the centre of each star, using yellow sewing thread.

5 Pin the purse together and use over stitch (see page 93) in red yarn to join up the side seams. Darn in all loose ends (see page 90) and remove the pins.

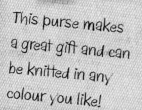

This purse makes a great gift and can be knitted in any colour you like!

PHONE CASE

Keep your phone safe and stylish with a cosy cover.

START HERE

Knitting pattern

FINISHED ITEM LAID FLAT MEASURES:
8 x 12 cm

PHONE CASE:

BEGIN: Cast on 19 stitches in blue yarn.

NEXT: Knit every row until your work measures 20 cm (garter stitch, see page 90).

END: Cast off.

STRAP (OPTIONAL):

BEGIN: Cast on 4 stitches in blue.

NEXT: Knit every row until strap measures 20 cm.

END: Cast off.

LAZY DAISY

Come up through the fabric and make a small loop. Then push the needle down next to where it came up. Come up again inside the top of the loop, and make a small stitch to hold it in place. Repeat for each petal.

YOU WILL NEED:

- Blue DK yarn
- A small quantity of yellow DK yarn
- A small quantity of white DK yarn
- 4 mm knitting needles
- A yellow button
- Black sewing thread
- 15 mm snap fastener
- Darning needle
- Sewing needle
- Round end pins
- Tape measure
- Scissors

13 cm

1 Measure 13 cm from the cast off edge and fold the fabric up. Fold over the top flap and sew the yellow button in the centre, using the darning needle.

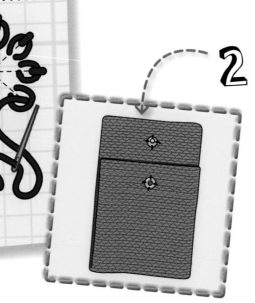

2 Sew the top of the snap fastener onto the underside of the flap, under the button. Sew the bottom of the snap fastener below the flap. Make sure that it lines up with the top fastener.

3 Use white yarn to embroider flower petals on the top flap using lazy daisy stitch.

4 Pin the case together and stitch up the side seams using over stitch (see page 93) and the blue yarn. Remove the pins.

5 Pin each end of the strap to the sides of the phone case. Sew on using over stitch and blue yarn to finish. Darn in all loose ends and remove the pins.

You could sew a felt or fabric shape onto your phone case instead of embroidering it. Sew on any extra details, such as eyes.

CORSAGE BROOCH

Jazz up your outfit with this knitted brooch. You can knit it in one or two colours.

YOU WILL NEED:

- DK yarn in two different colours
- 4 mm knitting needles
- Darning needle
- Embroidery or sewing needle
- Green felt
- A brooch back
- Dark green embroidery thread
- An air erasable fabric pen or tailor's chalk
- Pencil, paper and scissors

START HERE

Knitting pattern

FINISHED ITEM MEASURES: 5 x 5 cm

TWO COLOUR BROOCH:

BEGIN: Cast on 60 stitches in yarn A. Cut the yarn 30 cm from the needle.

NEXT: Join with yarn B (see page 90). Knit 5 rows.

ROW 6: Knit 2 together (see page 92). Repeat this until the end of the row. (30 stitches left.)

ROW 7: Work the same as the previous row. (15 stitches left.)

END: Cast off. Leave 60 cm of yarn for sewing up.

To knit a single colour brooch follow the same pattern but do not cut the yarn or add a new yarn.

1 Thread the tail of yarn B onto the darning needle. With the cast off edge face up, roll the fabric. As you roll, darn the fabric together along the edge, using over stitch (see page 93). Darn in the end. Turn the piece over and thread the tail of yarn A through to the back of the corsage.

2 Draw a leaf shape on the paper. Use it as a template to cut out two felt leaves. Draw veins onto the leaves, using the fabric pen or chalk.

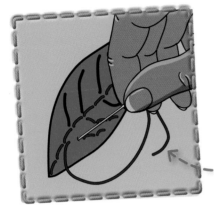

3 Split the embroidery thread so that you have two sets of three strands. Darn the veins onto the leaves using back stitch (see page 93).

4 Sew the leaves onto the back of the flower, using over stitch and embroidery thread.

5 Use the loose yarn from step 1 and over stitch to attach a brooch back. Darn in the loose ends.

Use your brooches to decorate hats and clothes for a vintage look.

SUGAR PLUM CUSHION

This mini cushion is easy to knit and makes a cute present.

YOU WILL NEED:

- 2 x 100 g/137 m balls of pink chunky yarn (that uses 6.5 mm knitting needles)
- A small quantity of lime green chunky yarn
- 6.5 mm knitting needles
- 25.5 x 25.5 cm (10 inch) cushion pad
- Dark and pale pink felt
- 3 buttons and a small quantity of DK yarn
- Darning needle
- Round end pins
- Tape measure
- Pencil, paper and scissors

START HERE

Knitting pattern

TENSION SQUARE PATTERN:

Knit a tension square (see page 93) by casting on 18 stitches and knitting 24 rows in stocking stitch (see page 90).
Pattern gauge: 14 stitches x 19 rows

FINISHED ITEM LAID FLAT MEASURES:
25.5 x 25.5 cm

CUSHION:

BEGIN: Cast on 36 stitches in pink yarn.

NEXT: Work stocking stitch (see page 90) until your work measures 74 cm.

END: Cast off.

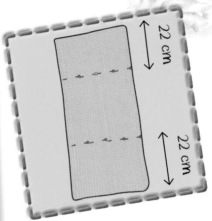

22 cm
22 cm

1 Insert two lines of pins 22 cm from the top and bottom edges of the fabric. This marks out the square on the front where you will embroider the flowers.

2 Draw an 8 x 8 cm flower on some paper and cut it out. Use this as a template to cut three flowers out of felt.

3 Pin the flowers onto the top of the fabric. Using DK yarn and a darning needle, sew a button over each flower and through the back of the fabric. Remove the pins from the felt.

4 Embroider stems and leaves for each flower using lime green chunky yarn and back stitch (see page 93). Remove the two lines of pins.

5 Fold the top back 22 cm so that the front is on the inside. Pin and sew up the side seams using over stitch (see page 93). Repeat this with the bottom section. Remove the pins and darn in the loose ends. Turn the cushion right side out and insert the pad.

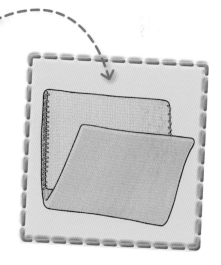

Use your felt and yarn to create any shape or design. How about some fish in an ocean scene or just a crazy pattern?

BEADED SCARF

Accessorize a simple knitted scarf with beads and tassels.

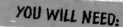

START HERE

Knitting pattern

TENSION SQUARE PATTERN:

Knit a tension square (see page 93) by casting on 16 stitches and knitting 25 rows in garter stitch (see page 90).

Pattern gauge: 12 stitches × 21 rows

FINISHED ITEM LAID FLAT MEASURES:

16 × 150 cm (excluding tassels)

BEADED SCARF:

BEGIN: Cast on 20 stitches in turquoise yarn.

NEXT: Work garter stitch (see page 90) until your work measures 150 cm.

END: Cast off.
Darn in all loose ends.

Use the pattern on page 104 to make a matching hat.

1 Cut 38 pieces of lime green yarn, each 70 cm long. Hold two lengths of yarn and loop them in half. Use the crochet hook to pull the loop between the first and second 'v' knit stitches on the scarf.

2 Thread the yarn ends through the loop you just made and pull firmly to secure.

3 Do this for the remaining 18 spaces. Repeat steps 1 to 3 on the other end of the scarf.

4 Make a knot in the tassel and use the darning needle to thread on a bead. Knot the yarn under the bead to keep it in place.

5 Add as many beads as you want and then trim all the tassels to the same length.

Add a different colour yarn (see page 90) to make a striped scarf in the colours of your favourite sports team.

BEAR HAT

You'll never want to leave home without this furry friend.

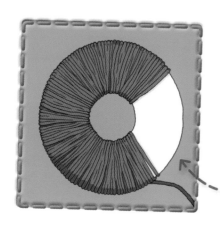

1 Cut two identical 4.5 cm cardboard rings. Wrap the brown yarn around the ring until the hole in the middle is very tight.

2 Cut the yarn along the edge, between the cardboard rings. Pass a length of yarn between the cardboard rings and tie it tightly. Remove the cardboard. Make another ear in the same way and sew both onto the hat.

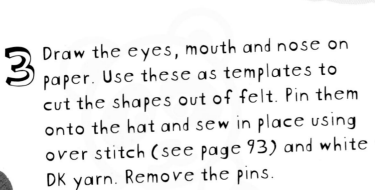

3 Draw the eyes, mouth and nose on paper. Use these as templates to cut the shapes out of felt. Pin them onto the hat and sew in place using over stitch (see page 93) and white DK yarn. Remove the pins.

Knitting pattern

TENSION SQUARE PATTERN:

Knit a tension square (see page 93) by casting on 18 stitches and knitting 24 rows in stocking stitch (see page 90).

Pattern gauge: 14 stitches × 19 rows

FINISHED ITEM WILL FIT:

53 cm head circumference

ANIMAL HAT:

BEGIN: Cast on 66 stitches in beige yarn.

ROW 1: Knit 2 stitches, purl 2 stitches and repeat this to the end of the row. Knit 2 stitches.

ROW 2: Purl 2 stitches, knit 2 stitches and repeat until the end of the row. Purl 2 stitches.

ROWS 3 and 4: Work as rows 1 and 2.

NEXT: Work 16 rows or 9 cm in stocking stitch ending on a purl row. If you want a longer hat add more rows in multiples of two.

DECREASING:
ROW 1: Knit 6 stitches, knit 2 together (see page 92). Repeat 8 times. Knit 2 stitches. (58 stitches left.)

ROW 2: Purl this row and every following even row (4, 6, 8, 10, 12, 14).

ROW 3: Knit 5 stitches, knit 2 together. Repeat 8 times. Knit 2 stitches. (50 stitches left.)

ROW 5: Knit 4 stitches, knit 2 together. Repeat 8 times. Knit 2 stitches. (42 stitches left.)

ROW 7: Knit 3 stitches, knit 2 together. Repeat 8 times. Knit 2 stitches. (34 stitches left.)

ROW 9: Knit 2 stitches, knit 2 together. Repeat 8 times. Knit 2 stitches. (26 stitches left.)

ROW 11: Knit 1 stitch, knit 2 together. Repeat 8 times. Knit 2 stitches. (18 stitches left.)

ROW 13: Knit 2 together. Repeat this until the end of the row. (9 stitches left.)

END: Cut the yarn approximately 30 cm from the needle. Thread the tail onto a darning needle and pass each stitch from your knitting needle to the darning needle. Then pull the yarn through firmly and darn in the loose end (see page 90).

4 Embroider a couple of white over stitches onto each eye. Embroider the mouth features in black DK yarn, using back stitch (see page 93).

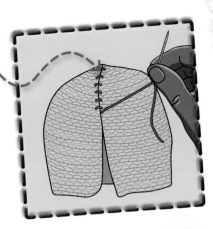

EGG COSY

A bunny egg cosy looks as cute as can be on your breakfast table!

1 Turn the cosy inside out. Sew the seam using over stitch (see page 93). Darn in the loose ends.

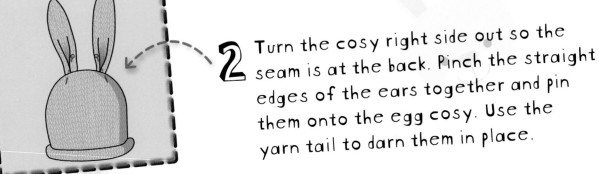

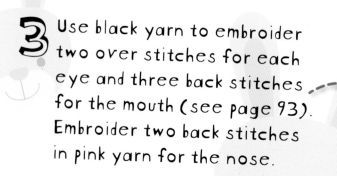

2 Turn the cosy right side out so the seam is at the back. Pinch the straight edges of the ears together and pin them onto the egg cosy. Use the yarn tail to darn them in place.

3 Use black yarn to embroider two over stitches for each eye and three back stitches for the mouth (see page 93). Embroider two back stitches in pink yarn for the nose.

Knitting pattern

FINISHED ITEM LAID FLAT MEASURES:
6 x 10 cm (including the ears)

EGG COSY:

BEGIN: Cast on 42 stitches in pale blue yarn.

NEXT: Work stocking stitch (see page 90) for 20 rows.

DECREASING:

ROW 21: Knit 1 stitch, knit 2 together. Repeat this until the end of the row. (28 stitches left.)

ROW 22: Purl this row.

ROW 23: Knit 2 together. Repeat this until the end of the row. (14 stitches left.)

ROW 24: Purl this row.

END: Draw the yarn through the stitches (see page 105).

EARS (MAKE TWO)

BEGIN: Cast on 10 stitches in pale blue yarn.

NEXT: Work stocking stitch for 12 rows.

ROW 13: Knit 1 stitch, knit 2 together. Knit 4 stitches, knit 2 together. Knit 1 stitch. (8 stitches left.)

ROW 14: Purl this row and every following even row (16, 18).

ROW 15: Knit 1 stitch, knit 2 together. Knit 2 stitches, knit 2 together. Knit 1 stitch. (6 stitches left.)

ROW 17: Knit 1 stitch, knit 2 together twice. Knit 1 stitch. (4 stitches left.)

ROW 19: Knit 2 together twice. (2 stitches left.)

END: Draw the yarn through the stitches.

Make a chick using yellow yarn. Cut out a beak and two wings in yellow felt and sew onto the cosy using yellow thread.

MUG WARMER

Keep your drink hot with a personalized knitted mug warmer.

Knitting pattern

FINISHED ITEM LAID FLAT MEASURES:
26 x 9 cm (to fit a standard 26 x 10 cm mug)

BEGIN: Cast on 58 stitches in pale pink yarn.

ROW 1: Knit 1 stitch, purl 1 stitch.
Repeat this until the end of the row.

NEXT: Repeat row 1 until your work measures 9 cm.

END: Cast off.

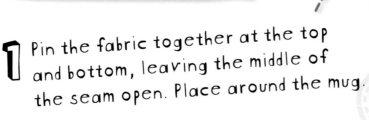

1 Pin the fabric together at the top and bottom, leaving the middle of the seam open. Place around the mug.

2 Draw a heart on the paper, about 7 x 6 cm. Cut it out and pin it onto the red felt.

3 Cut out the heart from the felt and pin it onto the cosy.

4 Carefully remove the fabric from the mug. Using cream DK yarn, stitch the heart onto the warmer with running stitch (see page 93). Remove the pins.

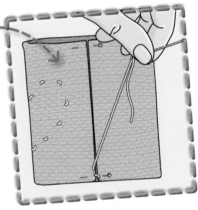

5 Turn the cosy inside out and re-pin the top and bottom seams. Sew a 1 cm seam at the top and bottom using over stitch (see page 93). Darn in the loose ends. Turn the cosy right side out.

You can use felt to create any design. How about a butterfly or a star? Or even the first letter of your name?

MINI HANDBAG

Complete your outfit with a stylish mini handbag.

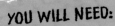

1 With the right sides facing inwards, pin the seams of the two bag pieces together. Sew the bottom and side seams up using over stitch (see page 93). Remove the pins and turn the bag right side out.

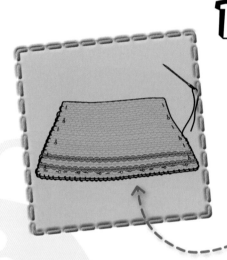

2 Pin the handles onto the bag and sew them on using over stitch. Remove the pins.

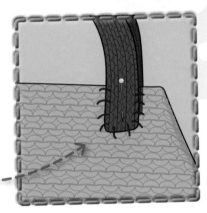

3 On paper, draw a flower about 8 x 8 cm. Use this as a template to cut a flower out of felt. Pin the flower onto the bag. Sew the button onto the felt flower and the bag. Remove the pins.

Knitting pattern

FINISHED ITEM LAID FLAT MEASURES:
22 × 23 cm (excluding the handles)

BAG SIDES (MAKE TWO):

BEGIN: Cast on 44 stitches in lilac yarn.

ROWS 1 TO 6: Work garter stitch (see page 90) for 6 rows.

DECREASING:

ROW 7: (Right side) Join with blue yarn. Knit 2 stitches, knit 2 together. Knit to last 4 stitches, knit 2 together, knit 2 stitches. (42 stitches left.)

ROW 8: Knit this row. Cut the yarn 30 cm from the needle.

ROWS 9 TO 12: Join with lilac yarn and knit 5 rows.

ROWS 13 AND 14: Work as rows 7 and 8. (40 stitches left.)

ROWS 15 TO 18: Work as rows 9 to 12.

ROW 19: Knit 2 stitches, knit 2 together. Knit to last 4 stitches, knit 2 together, knit 2 stitches. (38 stitches left.)

ROWS 20 TO 24: Knit 5 rows.

ROWS 25 TO 30: Work as rows 19 to 24. (36 stitches left.)

ROWS 31 TO 36: Work as rows 19 to 24. (34 stitches left.)

ROWS 37 TO 42: Work as rows 19 to 24. (32 stitches left.)

END: Cast off.

HANDLES (MAKE TWO):

BEGIN: Cast on 7 stitches in blue yarn.

ROW 1: Knit a stitch, purl a stitch. Repeat to the end of the row, ending with a knit stitch.

NEXT: Work as row 1 until your work measures about 32 cm.

END: Cast off.

Leave out the handles to turn your handbag into a stylish clutch bag. Sew snap fasteners onto the inside of the bag and cover these stitches with a button, bead or felt.

HAND WARMERS

Keep your wrists and hands warm with these toasty fingerless gloves.

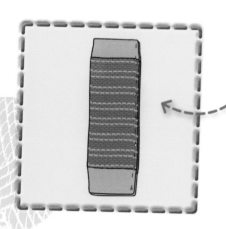

1 Take one knitted piece and fold it over so that the right side is facing inwards. Pin along the seam. Repeat with the other piece.

2 On the first piece, darn a 5 cm top seam, using over stitch (see page 93). Darn in the end. Leave 5 cm of the seam open for the thumb hole. Darn a 10 cm bottom seam using over stitch. Repeat on the second piece.

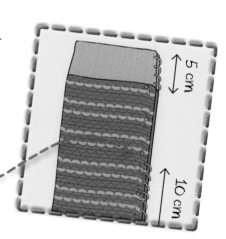

5 cm

10 cm

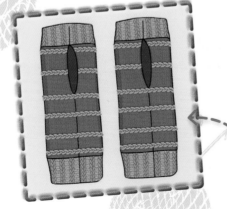

3 Remove the pins from both pieces. Darn in the loose ends and turn the hand warmers right side out.

Knitting pattern

TENSION SQUARE PATTERN:

Knit a tension square (see page 93) by casting on 26 stitches and knitting 32 rows in stocking stitch (see page 90).
Pattern gauge: 22 stitches × 28 rows

FINISHED ITEM LAID FLAT MEASURES:
9 × 20 cm (or 10 × 20 cm)

HAND WARMER (MAKE TWO):

Begin: Cast on 38 stitches (42 for bigger hands) in pale pink yarn.

RIB:

ROW 1: Knit 2 stitches, purl 2 stitches. Repeat this until the end of the row.

ROW 2: Purl 2 stitches, knit 2 stitches. Repeat this until the end of the row.

ROWS 3 TO 10: Work as rows 1 and 2, four times.

ROWS 11 AND 12: Knit 2 rows. Cut the yarn, leaving a 30 cm length for sewing up.

MAIN PATTERN:

ROWS 13 TO 16: Join with the turquoise yarn (see page 90) and work 4 rows in stocking stitch. Do not cut the yarn.

ROWS 17 AND 18: Join with the pale pink yarn and knit 2 rows. Cut the yarn leaving a 30 cm length for sewing up.

PATTERN REPEAT:

ROWS 19 TO 22: Pick up turquoise yarn and work 4 rows in stocking stitch. Do not cut the yarn.

ROWS 23 AND 24: Join with pink yarn and knit 2 rows. Cut the yarn, leaving a 30 cm length for sewing up.

ROWS 25 TO 54. Repeat rows 19 to 24 five times. Do not cut the yarn on row 54.

RIB:

Work as rows 1 and 2 (three times).
(60 rows worked.)

END: Cast off.

Hand warmers are a great idea if you have cold hands but still need to use your fingers!

HEADBAND

This stylish headband looks great and keeps your ears warm!

Knitting pattern

TENSION SQUARE PATTERN:

Knit a tension square (see page 93) by casting on 16 stitches and knitting 25 rows in stocking stitch (see page 90). Pattern gauge: 22 stitches × 28 rows

FINISHED ITEM SIZE:

Measure around your head and knit a piece 2 cm shorter than your measurement. It will be roughly 53 cm.

HEADBAND:

BEGIN: Cast on 22 stitches in blue yarn.

ROW 1: Knit this row. (This will be the right side.)

ROW 2: Knit 3 stitches, purl 16 stitches, knit 3 stitches.

NEXT: Repeat rows 1 and 2 until your work is the length you need.

END: Cast off. Cut the yarn, leaving approximately 50 cm for sewing up the seam.

YOU WILL NEED:

- A 100 g/280 m ball of blue DK yarn (that uses 4 mm knitting needles)
- A small quantity of white DK yarn
- 4 mm knitting needles
- Darning needle
- Round end pins
- Turquoise felt
- Button
- 1.5 m of thin ribbon
- Tape measure
- Pencil, paper and scissors

1 Fold over the fabric so that the right side is inside and pin along the side seam.

2 Sew the seam up using over stitch (see page 93). Darn in the loose ends. Remove the pins. Turn the fabric right side out.

3 Thread the ribbon onto the darning needle. Starting at the seam, sew the ribbon around the headband, using running stitch (see page 93). Make sure you sew the ribbon inside the textured edge.

4 Put the headband on and tie the ribbon ends together in a bow. Remove the headband.

5 On paper, draw a flower about 8 x 8 cm. Use it as a template to cut the same shape out of the felt. Pin the flower onto the headband. Sew the button onto the felt flower and the headband. Remove the pins and darn in the loose ends.

This headband looks great in any colour. A different-coloured felt flower also looks stylish.

SQUISHY PENGUIN

This huggable penguin would look great perched by your bed!

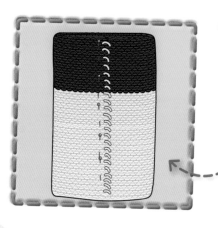

1 Fold the fabric over with the right side facing inwards. This will make a seam in the centre. Pin and sew up the seam using over stitch (see page 93). Remove the pins.

2 Sew running stitch (see page 93) around the cast off edge using the black yarn tail. Pull the yarn firmly to gather the fabric. Darn the edges and the yarn end in securely.

3 Turn the fabric right side out. Fill with toy stuffing. Repeat step 2 with the cream yarn.

eyes

beak   feet

4 On paper, draw two circles for the eyes, a triangle for the beak and two feet. Use these as templates to cut the shapes out of felt.

Knitting pattern

FINISHED ITEM MEASURES:
8 x 13 cm

HEAD AND BODY:

BEGIN: Cast on 50 stitches in cream yarn. Work stocking stitch (see page 90) until the work measures 9 cm and ends in a purl row. Cut the yarn 30 cm from the needle.

NEXT: Join with black yarn. Work stocking stitch until the work measures 13 cm and ends in a purl row.

END: Cast off.

WINGS (MAKE TWO)

BEGIN: Cast on 9 stitches in black yarn.

ROWS 1–14: Work stocking stitch for 14 rows.

DECREASING:

ROW 15: Knit 1 stitch, knit 2 together, knit 3 stitches, knit 2 together, knit 1 stitch. (7 stitches left.)

ROW 16: Purl this row and all other even rows (18, 20).

ROW 17: Knit 1 stitch, knit 2 together, knit 1 stitch, knit 2 together, knit 1 stitch. (5 stitches left.)

ROW 19: Knit 2 together, knit 1 stitch, knit 2 together. (3 stitches left.)

ROW 21: Knit 2 together, knit 1 stitch. (2 stitches left.)

END: Draw the yarn through the stitches (see page 105).

5 Sew the felt eyes onto the penguin using two back stitches (see page 93). Sew the wings on using over stitch. Sew on the beak and feet, using over stitches on each side. Darn in the loose ends.

To make a square toy, like this owl, skip steps 2 and 3 and sew a seam along the cast off edge. Knot several yarn lengths together to make ears.

INDEX

119

INDEX